Spiritual Fatherhood

Every Believer's Call to Intimacy and Fruitfulness

Steve Watson

Desert Rock Publishing
West Richland, Washington 99353 USA

Desert Rock Publishing
West Richland, Washington 99253 USA

Publication/Printing Information

Spiritual Fatherhood: Every Believer's Call to Intimacy and Fruitfulness
Copyright © 2008 by Steven Watson: First Printing

International Standard Book Number (ISBN):
ISBN - 13: - 978 - 0 - 9814566 - 1- 4
ISBN - 10: - 0 – 9814566 – 1 – 8

Names and certain details used throughout this book as illustrations have been changed to protect the privacy of those individuals.

Design and layout published by
Desert Rock Publishing
5700 Laurel Drive
West Richland, Washington 99353 USA

Cover Picture taken by Keziah Watson near Galway, Ireland

Printed in United States of America

Contact Information
Steven Watson Ministries
Email : stevenwatson1345@msn.com
Website: www.drf-church.org
Phone: 509-967-1345 or 509-943-1445

Forward

Where does one learn how to *become* a spiritual father? What makes some spiritual fathers fantastic, while others are mediocre at best? There are scores of books on the shelves of any bookstore that will tell you how to father, how to be a better father, or even how to be a father to your own father in his latter years. However, there are few books that help one understand the journey toward becoming a spiritual father, the three-tiered process from "children" to "young men" to "fathers" that the Apostle John writes about. Those at each stage have their own abilities and divinely given responsibilities, but it is almost as if the church assumes that one is automatically ready to father. Therefore few, if any, tell the process that God takes a man through to *become* a good father. In other words, the *becoming* is different than the *how*, and it is the manner in which we process through each stage that makes us good spiritual fathers.

Good spiritual fathers do not just happen. They must be taken through the eye of the needle, and that process is not an easy one. I am glad Steve Watson has written *Spiritual Fatherhood,* a book that helps one learn what God puts us through as He hones the man to become a spiritual father. God's work in the heart of a man to prepare him to love, develop, direct, and envision his children, whether they are natural or spiritual, is agonizing. To father anyone, choosing their good over our own well being, requires a change in spiritual DNA because our personal survival instincts are too strong. The ability to lead his children from the viewpoint of hope for their tomorrow rather than of fear of their failure does not come cheaply. Only a true spiritual father can do it.

A good spiritual father will have been prepared for his role long before the natural or spiritual child comes along. Once in that role, a good father never assumes he knows all there is about fathering, and so he is constantly in a state of learning and maturing even as he becomes a grandfather. Therefore, a good father begets good fathers who will do the same for those they father. It is a self-evident principle of the kingdom: "one begets what he is."

A good spiritual father carries the attributes of brokenness, patience, vision, faith, selflessness, meekness, gentleness, and a firm set of boundaries. The price paid to acquire these attributes is beyond the scope one would volunteer for, but the satisfaction and sense of personal fulfillment far exceed the cost. Yes, there is always more understanding to be gleaned, more wisdom to be found, and more knowledge to acquire, but the fact that you are reading this book promises that you've now come to the point where you will not fail. You are simply honing those fathering skills that the Lord spent a lot of time preparing you to use. Isn't it time to do it?

John Paul Jackson
Author and Spiritual Father

Honoring Fathers and Friends

I said goodbye to Charlie today, along with about 300 or 400 of his friends and family. It is hard to believe he is gone. How does Superman die? How do I ever thank him for loving me and seeing in me what no one else did? How do I check in with him, partly to see how he is doing, partly to show him how well I am doing so he could be proud of me? Questions like these flooded my mind as I sat listening to one "spiritual son" after another give testimony to the impact that Charlie had on their lives. The funeral had lasted close to two and a half hours already, and I was amazed at how many people seemed content to listen to and agree with each testimony.

The place was packed and this was the third funeral service for Charlie in as many locations. There had been one in Canada where Charlie served his fourth and final church, one on the Oregon Coast where he had pastored his second church, and now this one in Portland, Oregon where he had pastored his third church. What a legacy this man left behind though never pastoring a church of more than 200 or 300 people.

I was about 12 years old when I met Charlie Fischer. We met at Bible Baptist Church in Astoria, Oregon, which was his first senior pastorate after he had been our youth pastor for a few years. Charlie and Kaye, his wife, were unbelievably passionate about Jesus the day I met them and still were the last time I saw them, 35 years later in the summer of 2006. Our family had gone up to Canada to spend time with them, not realizing it would be our final visit with Charlie.

While there we rode horses, made s'mores in their backyard fire pit, and lost at cards to them yet again. It felt like we were catching up and saying good-bye all at the same time. Charlie told me things he had never shared before about the churches he and Kaye had pastored and about the spiritual warfare they had endured. He spoke of his regrets and of his hopes for the future. I reminded him of the time he took me hiking at the ocean and how he showed me all kinds of sea critters in the tide pools along the rock formations. We also laughed about how he kicked me out of youth group for being a rebellious disrupter of everything good and holy. I was a senior in high school and had just become involved in the drug world, though he had no idea about that. A year and a half later he restored me and appointed me youth pastor. I had never understood why he did the things he did to help and encourage me, but over the years I began to realize that Charlie was my spiritual father. He helped birth me into the things of the kingdom, nurtured me in my walk, and then sent me out to minister. The values he instilled in me are still present today. The way he treated me is the way I treat people, and the passion he had for the Lord I now carry.

Our family trip to Canada was definitely different because Charlie seemed to tire more easily. He had always been a bundle of energy and enthusiasm. Little did we know he would suffer his first heart attack a couple of months after we left and would die of a massive heart attack four months later on February 21, 2007.

Charlie was my hero. When they came to pastor our little Baptist church, he and Kaye blew us away with their devotion to God and their "hand raising" during worship, which was a little controversial for a Conservative Baptist church in the early 1970s. Their love for the Lord was deeper than any I had ever seen or experienced. When I learned Charlie had come from difficult circumstances, it gave me hope that I, too, would be able to rise above mine. In Charlie, I could see hope for myself as I struggled with the shame and fear that comes from living in an alcoholic's home.

Sometimes you don't appreciate people the way you should, and I certainly failed to realize what gifts Charlie and Kaye were to us until I started to grow up and take on similar responsibilities.

Pastoring a church is the hardest thing I have ever done. Doing it right is even harder. Some of us struggle with being a little too self-focused, but Charlie had learned how to be a true spiritual father. Spiritual fathers are all about raising up sons and daughters who walk out their destinies with confidence, knowing that they are loved and supported. They are more interested in seeing people move into their callings than in protecting and promoting their own ministries.

As we drove away from the Portland church where Charlie's memorial service was held, I resolved in my heart to write this book. I have been graced by God to have men like Charlie Fischer, Tom Miller, John Paul Jackson, John Sanford and Denny Cline help me along the way. These men have grown into spiritual maturity and authority and they are recognized as spiritual fathers by those who encounter them. As saints, some are well known and some are hidden, but they are all worth emulating.

Tom Miller is a retired detective and pastor from Kansas. God crossed our paths at the beginning of my own spiritual Pentecost, and Tom has remained a constant presence since. Tom has treated me with respect and kindness as he helped me get a backbone, see truth for what it is, and find a sense of humor when life seemed overwhelming. He has faithfully called to check in on me since we met in June 1997. Tom has allowed me to grow without shame, ask questions without fear, and to share with him what I am learning as I grow into my calling and destiny. Tom is a very humble man, and he has the sort of character you hope a mature father would have. I can always count on him to be straight with me, as well as being kind and gentle. I thank God for Tom and his wife, Pricilla. They are true fathers and mothers in the kingdom.

I received my first training in the prophetic by John Paul Jackson through his courses, "The Art of Hearing God" and "Advanced Prophetic Ministry". Pam and I have been astonished by how freely he has poured his love and insight into us and our leaders. He has been wonderfully open and humble. His willingness to be transparent with us has helped us gain confidence to lead; his kindness and gentleness is Christ- like and genuine. John Paul has taught us to be kingdom minded and to hear God's voice. He is truly a spiritual father, mentor, and a man to be honored.

I met John Sanford in June of 1997 in an Elijah House Prayer Counseling School, where I also met Tom Miller. Those three weeks changed my life. I had been a pastor and counselor for a number of years in a megachurch, but I had never been filled with the Holy Spirit. During that three- week period, I had numerous experiences with the Holy Spirit that would propel me to plant Desert Rock Fellowship two and a half years later. At Desert Rock, we had the pleasure of having John do a conference for us in the summer of 2004, during which he prayed a father's blessing over Pam and I that we will never forget.

We used John's tape series on inner healing every Wednesday night for the first several months of our church's existence, and it impacted us beyond what we could have hoped for. We watched people learn to minister to each other as God began to heal deep wounds. John and Paula are true pioneers in the inner healing movement and we love and respect them for their contributions to us and to the body of Christ.

I met Denny and Ann Cline in November 2002 when they invited a friend and me to attend a conference at their church. Denny and Ann pastor the Albany Vineyard in Oregon. I consider that place a second home.

Denny is a pastor I want to emulate because he fearlessly pursues the presence of God and carries a regional anointing for fathering people like me, pastors who look for continual encouragement to keep going. Denny and Ann have embraced Pam and me in such a loving way that we cannot deny that we have value to God and a place in the kingdom. Pam and I don't have words enough to express our love and thanks to the Clines.

I want to thank a few others. To my dad, Gordon Watson, thank you for coming to my football and basketball games, for teaching me to golf, and for encouraging me to be a man of character.

To my mom, Pat Coalman, thank you for birthing me and praying me into the kingdom. I know I got some of my fire and passion from you, and I am grateful for it.

To my stepfather, Lee Coalman, thank you for showing me what it means to lay down your life for your wife and children. You have been an incredible example to me, and if you keep praying, I might get there.

To my wife, Pam, thank you! I am so blessed to have you in my life. Pam, you are a great wife and partner. Thank you for blessing me with your love and patience. You are an encouragement and my favorite!

To Keziah, Ian, Andrew, and Autumn, I love you! I am so proud of each of you and I can't wait to see what happens in your lives as you grow from young men and women into fathers and mothers in the kingdom. You all have incredible destinies and your Mom and I are rooting for you to run the race and win the prize.

To Duane and Karen Smith, thank you for your friendship and the use of your lake cabin so I could write. Thank you for helping to direct and develop our missions vision. You are lifesavers!

To George and Jane Westsik, Martin and Felicia Iedema and Jim and Cody Allen, thank you all for helping me oversee

9

Desert Rock Fellowship. Your faithfulness inspires me, and your love will reap great rewards.

To Roger and Rebecca Kohlas, thank you for your love and high regard for me. Your desire to help me financially to edit this book was an incredible and needed gift. Your friendship and leadership role with the intercessors have taken us to incredible heights.

To Lisa Ballou and Karin Spanner, thank you for your incredible work editing this book. I am forever grateful to you both and hope to work with you in the future.

To Ben Meyer, thank you for all of your hard work on the cover design. I am grateful for your heart and character and how they are reflected in your excellent work.

To the church affectionately called Desert Rock Fellowship, you are a reflection of God's grace to us and an expression of His bride that we are astounded to behold. Thank you for your patience and grace. We love you all!

Contents

Forward *3*

Honoring Fathers and Friends *5*

Introduction *13*

Part One
Growing from Spiritual Childhood to Spiritual Fatherhood in the Kingdom

Chapter 1

Coming Alive and Learning to Walk:
A Vision of the Maturity Process *17*

Chapter 2

Fathering Is About the Heart:
Our Hearts Need Renewal *29*

Chapter 3

Walking in the Father's Blessing:
Character Formation *37*

Part Two
What Spiritual Young Men Learn: Spiritual Discernment, Application of the Word and How to Overcome Their Enemies

Chapter 4

Acquiring Discernment and Wisdom:
Learning to hear God's Voice *51*

Chapter 5

Overcoming Persecution, Abuse, and Fear:
Dealing with Offense.. *65*

Chapter 6

Overcoming Personal Strongholds:
Learning to Apply Truth.. *75*

Chapter 7

Overcoming Corporate Strongholds:
Learning to Strengthen Yourself and Others.......................... *85*

Part Three
What Fathers Do: How to Father, What to Teach and Model

Chapter 8

Understanding Your Calling and Mission:
Getting and Keeping a Clear Purpose *101*

Chapter 9

Fathering, Mentoring, and Leading:
Tools for Nurturing Others *109*

Chapter 10

Spiritual Lessons that Season:
Growing them up Right... *123*

Appendix.. *135*
Discussion Questions for Small Groups........................*140*

Introduction

This book is intended for every believer. It isn't a "for pastor's only" book. Spiritual fatherhood and motherhood is the call on every believer's life. I will refer to spiritual fatherhood often, but please note I refer to all believers. God has a ministry for every one of you. Doing ministry from a place of intimacy and maturity will bear lasting fruit. This is God's best plan for you.

I am not writing this book from a perspective of strength. I don't feel qualified to write on this topic, but I am called to do so. I believe the Lord has given me insights into the process of how He takes us from spiritual children to spiritual fathers. I have ministered overseas, trained pastors, planted churches and dealt with plenty of trouble in life and ministry. I have had some experiences with the Lord that will hopefully help you understand His love and grace as you walk through His winnowing process of maturing you.

In telling my story I have covered the identity of those God has used to refine me by being vague or disguising some of the details. For those of you who know me, let love and God's grace cover us. I share the details I do because in my careful analysis of what I felt was appropriate (with the counsel of several others) I saw some life lessons from which others might benefit.

This book is divided into three distinct sections. The first section is an overview of the maturity process that God takes all of us through, if we are willing. It covers the growth process believers experience from being a spiritual child to becoming a spiritual father, including what we know when we are born again and how our hearts and character are formed.

The second section of the book focuses on what spiritual young men learn on their way to becoming spiritual fathers.

Spiritual young men learn the Word of God and how to overcome in spiritual warfare. I spend time discussing how we learn to hear God's voice, gain discernment and how to deal with spiritual strongholds. The third and final section presents the role of a spiritual father, including how to teach and model Christ.

My hope in writing is that more men and women will feel compelled to take up the mandate to move on from spiritual childhood and to become true spiritual fathers and mothers in His kingdom. May God bless you as you read about and consider your calling.

Part One

Growing from Spiritual Childhood to Spiritual Fatherhood in the Kingdom

Chapter 1

Coming Alive and Learning to Walk

"I write to you, little children,
Because your sins are forgiven you
for His name's sake.
I write to you, fathers,
Because you have known Him who is
from the beginning.
I write to you, young men,
Because you have overcome the
wicked one.
I write to you, little children,
Because you have known the Father.
I have written to you, fathers,
Because you have known Him who is
from the beginning.
I have written to you, young men,
Because you are strong, and the
Word of God abides in you,
And you have overcome the wicked
one.

1 John 2:12-14

A Vision of the Maturity Process

In February1998, I had a vision lasting about two and a half hours that beautifully illustrated the maturity process of believers that is described in the Scripture above. When I received this vision, my wife Pam and I were at Elijah House for a week receiving counseling. In the room were Pam, our counselor, an intern, and myself. During the vision, my counselor saw what I was seeing. I don't know why God did that, but we experienced the same vision at the same time. Prior to arriving at Elijah House, I had been on a 40-day Daniel fast that was to end as we finished our counseling that day. As we prepared to pray before the session was to begin, I heard the Lord say to me, "Jeremiah 33:3." I had no idea what that verse was, so I handed my Bible to Pam and asked her to look it up and read it. Here is what she read:

"Call to me, and I will answer you, and show you great and mighty things, which you do not know."

Obviously this sounded promising. The next thing I knew I was in a vision. I saw Jesus come to get me out of miry clay. I was in a very dark place. I was a small emaciated child. I was wearing a dirty, white, night shirt. He took me to a pool of water, and He washed me off. He then baptized me and gave me a drink. As He did this, I noticed that a transformation was taking place. I was no longer a small child, but had matured to a boy about eight years old. I was now wearing an altar boy robe. I found this extremely puzzling as I had no Catholic background whatsoever. At this stage in the vision, I was doing very rudimentary types of Christian service, like helping to pass out communion elements.

As the vision progressed, I eventually began to carry out ministry and spiritual warfare in a foreign land. By this time I was wearing a Catholic priest's robe and appeared to be a young man somewhere between 20 and 30 years old. Toward the end of the vision, I saw myself transformed into an older man dressed in a Catholic cardinal's clothing and hat. I was at the top of a hill or mountain, and I could see the lights of heaven in the distance. By the Holy Spirit's insight, I knew that I couldn't proceed on into heaven because there was something that God wanted me to see and do. As I turned to my left, I realized that I had climbed a mountain. It looked like one of those rolling hills you see in the

Scottish Highlands. There was a cobblestone path, which I had walked, that wound down and around the hillside and reappeared again before disappearing in the distance. Much to my surprise, the path was filled with hundreds, maybe thousands of people. I knew that I couldn't go into heaven until I had shown them the way in, so I stood at the top of the mountain and waved them on up the mountain and in to heaven. While I was still in the vision, I realized that these people were my spiritual inheritance. Then the vision ended.

In sharing this vision, I want you to focus on the maturity process that was revealed. The vision illustrates the Scripture quoted at the beginning of this chapter. First John 2:12-14 describes the stages of spiritual maturity. At any one point in this process, a believer is a child, a young man, or a father in the kingdom.

In the vision God was showing me the depth of His love for me as He found me, cleansed me, and cared for me. The Catholic symbolism revealed that there would be various spiritual levels in my life that He would define. He wanted me to understand that though I had had limitations early in life, if I followed the path He set for me, I would be very fruitful. Let's look at the passage of Scripture again and see if we can develop a greater understanding of God's defined process of maturity.

According to oral tradition, 1 John 2:12-14 was often quoted or sung during Christian gatherings much like the Apostle's Creed was later on in the church's history. These verses sum up a three-stage maturity process that is both simple and profound. We know from this passage of Scripture and from John 3:16 that there are two basic foundational truths that mark new converts. As children in the faith, we come to understand that we are loved by God the Father and Jesus, His Son, and that our sins are forgiven through Jesus' sacrifice on the cross. These two truths define not only a basic foundation for our faith, but they also give hope and new life through a born again experience. In this first stage, being

19

defined as a child in the faith has nothing to do with chronological age. It is simply a picture of the new relationship we have with God. We all start out as children, yet God desires that we progress past childhood and on into maturity and intimacy.

In the second stage, young men in the faith have progressed to another level of spiritual understanding and authority. They are busy learning the Word of God and using it to wage successful spiritual warfare. They are marked by an ever increasing strength and ability to overcome the wicked one because the Word of God abides in them. Children in the kingdom know they can continually come to the Father to have their sins forgiven, while young men learn to overcome the enemy and with the Holy Spirit's help, break down strongholds in their lives. Once they are able to experience a level of freedom for themselves, they are able to bring hope and deliverance to others.

As children grow into young men in the kingdom, they watch and learn from those who are more mature in the faith. These are the fathers, those in the third stage of maturity. A father's passion for the Lord should demonstrate itself in worship and ministry that flow from a place of intimate love. A true spiritual father's relationship with God tends to inspire and motivate others to pursue their own intimate relationship with Him. Intimacy is gained through spending time with God. Fathers have gained an understanding of God's heart for people, and they lay down their lives for others.

What differentiates a father from a young man or child is experiential in nature. The word for "father" in this passage is *pater* in the Greek language, which means father, mentor or model, as in role model, like Jesus is to us. The passage we are looking at repeats twice that fathers have "known" Him. The word translated as "known" is *ginosko* in the Greek language and has the connotation of being able to recognize, understand, or to have sexual relations with. This type of "knowing" is very intimate. In the natural realm you have to be intimate to become a father or mother. The same is true in the spiritual realm.

There are differences between how a child, a young man, or a mature father approach God, and how believers in these stages relate to Him. In all three levels, believers can keep short accounts with God concerning sin and can understand His love for them. A young man and a father know the Word of God, understand how to overcome in spiritual warfare, and pass on their understanding to others. But only the spiritual father, the one who is intimate with our Heavenly Father, will know the ways of God in a more global sense. The true father will not only approach the Father in heaven for his own needs and the needs of others, but he will know how to minister to Him as well.

A father in the kingdom has the ability to enter into an intimate relationship where ministry flows between God and man. Though God doesn't need this intimacy, He delights in it much like a parent does when his children sing his praises! During these times of sweet worship and meditation, the Heavenly Father reveals His heart to the heart of the spiritual father. At this level of relationship, a father will begin to hear God's heart for the kingdom and to gain insights concerning the needs of people and will be moved to share His burden in prayer. This burden bearing activity sometimes leads to instructions on how He would like His trusted friend to intervene when a member of His flock has trouble.

A father has experienced and understands the *intimate focus* and *longing* our God has for us. This *loving attention* reveals God's *care* in such a way that the intimates of God are able to return it to Him as they worship. By doing so, we minister to Him. God has shown us *acceptance,* which is His deliberate and ready reception of us. We have His *favor* and *appreciation,* which He enjoys to see us return to Him in praise. We have experienced His *encouragement* in times of trouble, and we have seen His *faithfulness* to us manifested in provision, grace, and mercy. He longs to see us be faithful to Him and to His kingdom. God is blessed when we acknowledge His faithfulness while diligently being faithful in return. God seeks to *honor* us (2 Timothy 2:20-21) as we humble ourselves in love for His service, and He is blessed when we honor Him with our mouths and actions in worship. God has gone out of His way to convey His *affection* for us. When we return this love, He is blessed. These are just a few of the ways a spiritual father learns to minister to the Holy One.

I have seen spiritual mothers and fathers in all kinds of church and social settings. Their fruit gives them away. They are the ones who quickly engage in worship when the opportunity arises. They carry God's perspective when difficult circumstances arise, while having faith in His ability to work things out for His glory and for our good. The mature father and mother remain steadfast even when outcomes aren't what people desired or hoped for. This is because they have spiritual understanding and "know" Him and His ways.

Spiritual mothers and fathers are the ones who support their pastors, even though they themselves could probably do a better job of it! Their support is evident because they know the ways of God, and they are confident that He is able to heal, discipline, and shape His leaders. Because of their deep trust in and love of God, they carry spiritual influence and favor wherever they go. The love they possess isn't showy, nor compulsively manufactured. Instead, it is genuine because it is born out of a life of intimacy with Him. Their love flows from their experiential understanding that God's love is not earned, but freely given and received. This allows the father and mother freedom from performing to earn God's favor and freedom from the fear of men. There is a "holy boldness" that comes to those who "know" Him and walk in the Spirit that powerfully affects their witness.

A few years ago, upon boarding a flight to Boston, my wife Pam and I were a little disappointed to find ourselves assigned to sit in the back of the plane. Our row mate was a young man who looked to be of Middle Eastern or Indian descent. Pam took the seat next to him, looking a little uncomfortable as he continually disregarded the flight attendant's instructions to end a call and to turn off his cell phone. After nearly losing his phone to the flight attendant, he finally hung up and then turned his gaze toward Pam. I began to pray for him as he engaged Pam in a dialogue about his life and religious history. Eventually, Pam pulled me into the conversation. He indeed was from India and had been visiting his girlfriend out West. He was a Hindu who had attended Catholic missionary schools when he was a young boy. He seemed to have a lot of questions and was confused about who God was and which religion was "right." As we listened and shared, I realized that he simply needed to experience God.

When I was a younger man, I would have tried to lead him through a tract, but in this particular situation doing that seemed inappropriate. The Lord has allowed me to experience His love and presence regularly, so I felt led to ask what seemed to him to be a very strange question, "Would you like to experience the peace and presence of God?" He got a funny look on his face and seemed to want more information. I explained to him that I carry the presence of God and if he would put his hand in mine, he could also experience God's peace and presence. He got a huge smile on his face and gingerly put his hand into mine. As soon as he did, I felt the peace of God come with warmth and joy. As he looked at me, his eyes got very large, his smile widened, and he blurted out, "Hey! You look just like Jesus!" (My wife stifled the urge to tell him right then and there that I was nothing like Him!) Pam and I laughed and told him that as a Christian your sins are forgiven, and you receive the presence of the Holy Spirit. He was thrilled that he could feel God's presence. After that a dynamic spiritual conversation ensued between the young man and my wife that lasted all the way from the West coast to the East coast. My work was done after our "little experiment," so I went back to playing games on my computer, knowing that God had this man's attention and was in hot pursuit.

This type of encounter is being repeated all the time by those who "know" and trust God. The world is waiting for the true bride of Christ to shine forth in beauty and holiness. When we seek to know God and to walk in the Spirit, He is faithful to help us become like Him. Just like the young man on the plane, those around us will see Jesus in our faces. To the nonreligious of His day, Jesus was very attractive. To the religious, He was a stumbling block. When an individual matures into a healthy father or mother in the kingdom, they become safe to approach because they are secure in their relationship with God. They carry the weight of faith and love through "knowing" Him and being known by Him that impacts any situation they encounter.

Looking back again at our Scripture focus for this chapter, I want to highlight some important insights about the maturity stages of a believer and maybe answer a few questions that may have arisen. The verses given for spiritual children indicate that they have some level of "knowing" God that I have defined as awareness at a relational level of His love for them and the availability of forgiveness for their sins. The verses that define young men in the kingdom indicate that they have learned the Word of God and have overcome the evil one while becoming spiritually "strong." As I described spiritual fathers, I focused on what they come to "know" about God. I have taken some liberty in describing what the spiritual father's journey looks like by examining some of my own experiences and those of others. I want to emphasize that hearing God's voice and worshipping Him aren't exclusively for spiritual fathers.

In the process of moving from spiritual childhood to fatherhood, everyone is invited to learn to hear God's voice and to worship Him at some level. Jesus told us that all of His sheep would hear His voice (John 10:4). In my experience, our depth of worship, our ability to hear God's voice, and the relationship we have with God, grow over time when the ingredients of faith and expectation are present. This is a supernatural work of the Holy Spirit that brings us into a deeper relationship with Him and moves us from being self-focused to being God-focused. There is friendship, revelation, and spiritual understanding about God and about the ongoing work of the kingdom that emerges and evolves over time for the spiritual father. The level of intimacy a person has with God isn't always congruent with the level of responsibility and influence they have in the organized church. Many men and women are promoted or promote themselves into positions of authority without proper healing and wholeness, not to mention intimacy with God, while many who are spiritual fathers and mothers quietly minister behind the scenes.

Those who walk in intimacy with God will tend to birth things in prayer and may be called to deliver timely words to individuals or groups that influence for good the health and fruitfulness of the body of Christ. Some may be simply set aside to minister to the Lord for seasons of their lives, while others may be moved into public ministries. Those who walk in the Spirit are recognized by the Spirit, whether they hold a humanly recognized spiritual office or not. And when I say they are recognized, I mean recognized by God, not necessarily men.

Recently there has been a proliferation of books and materials written on "leadership" that examine nearly everything but intimacy with God and walking in the Spirit. Often these books major on defining a leader's role, how to gain influence, and promoting a vision to be embraced by others. The authors so emphasize developing leadership "skills" that our real purpose of getting to "know Him" is lost.

Ephesians 4:11-13 tells us there are five gifts to the church: apostles, prophets, pastors, teachers, and evangelists. They are given by God to equip the church "until we all come to the unity of the faith and of the knowledge of the Son of God, to a perfect man, to the measure of the stature of the fullness of Christ . . ." Unfortunately, many people are so intent on attaining one of these positions or titles, that they forget the purpose of filling the role. Getting to know God and helping others do the same should be our goal, not gaining a position or title. A truly mature spiritual father will carry the ultimate apostolic burden found in Galatians 4:19:

"My little children, for whom I labor in birth again until Christ is formed in you . . ."

A true spiritual father's focus is on seeing *Christ* formed in people, not on gaining a reputation, a title, or even a recognized "full time ministry" position. I am astounded how my own heart has been exposed by God in this. At the beginning of this chapter, I shared a vision with you. It was a huge spiritual encounter for me. The thing I should have been most excited about was that I get to go to heaven at all (Luke 10:17-20). It wasn't. Instead, I was pumped about what I might get to see and do in my ministry in the future. Over the last few years, I have felt God ask me, "Am I enough?" The question unnerves me. He has asked me that question because it needed to be asked. Thankfully I haven't heard Him ask it recently.

I have learned that mature spiritual fathers long to be in His presence and to enjoy the intimacy of the "secret place" more than anything else. To desire ministry over intimacy reveals a priority set that is upside down. In my case, He has shown me future events that I long to be involved in. But I also know that there is some unhealthy ambition in me as well. I still have a desire to be known and appreciated. There is still some competitive drive in me to accomplish things that would permanently shut up some of my critics. I still find myself struggling with dissatisfaction and discontentment. All in all, though, I know that I am loved with an everlasting love and that He will carry me through to fulfill my life's call and destiny.

I am astounded by the number of "hidden" spiritual moms and dads that exist who receive profound revelation about global issues in the kingdom because they are intimate with God and because He has found them faithful. They aren't always the people standing up front speaking, and they aren't self-promoters. Yet,

26

those who walk in the Spirit recognize them when they do speak up. I want to be an intimate of God. My hope and prayer is that all of us do.

While fathers don't always have public ministries in the sense of pastoring or pioneering churches, it is a father's role to help birth, nurture, and send. When you get to a place of intimacy with God that has been cultivated over time, you conceive and give birth to the desires of God's heart. Whether this conception is revelation to pray in a revival or a burden to mentor someone who is younger in the faith, the intimacy you have with God will bear fruit. When God gives you revelation to birth, nurture, or send, you begin a process of fathering. Some fathers plant, some water, some fertilize, some weed, and some harvest. Whatever your fathering role, you are compelled by love to see Christ formed in people.

Many of you have probably seen a spiritually young man in the kingdom try to birth a ministry too soon. Though he is able to conceive and have a baby, he struggles with the care and nurture of it. Just as young parents in the natural struggle with a lack of wisdom and resources, so do those who father ministries too soon. Remember, chronological age isn't the issue here. Knowledge of the Word and winning personal victories in spiritual warfare don't necessarily qualify them to father in the kingdom. Without the requisite wisdom and experience in the ways of God, which bring understanding, a young man will fail to handle people and difficult circumstances with faith and skill. In the kingdom, even spiritual children can reproduce, but that doesn't mean they are ready to mentor!

In this chapter, we have taken a very brief look at the spiritual maturity process that every believer is called to go through. I have attempted to define spiritual children, young men, and fathers in the kingdom with a special emphasis on intimacy with God as the ultimate goal. Ministry becomes the fruit of intimacy in this model. In the next few chapters we will look at how God desires to renew our hearts and form our characters on the way to intimacy and spiritual fatherhood. As we go, I will present the process of maturing that God has carried me and others through with the hope that it will help and encourage you along your way. I find comfort in 2 Corinthians 9:8 and I hope you will too.

"And God is able to make all grace abound toward you, that you, always having all sufficiency in all things, may have an abundance for every good work."

CHAPTER 2

Fathering is About the Heart

"Behold, I will send you Elijah the
prophet
Before the coming of the great and
dreadful day of the Lord.
And he will turn
The hearts of the fathers to the
children,
And the hearts of the children to their
fathers,
Lest I come and strike the earth with
a curse."

Malachi 4:5-6

Our Hearts Need Renewal

I believe we are living in the days when the Holy Spirit is turning men's hearts to the children. He is also turning the hearts of the children to the fathers. I see the evidence. The generations behind us "baby boomers" are demanding real love and authentic relationship – a good thing! Spiritual fathers have responded with numerous schools of the spirit, internships, and mentoring programs. I have been excited to see churches include young men and women on their pastoral staffs, mission trips, and even on elder boards. I have watched the older women teach the younger ones how to pray, and I have seen young men show small children love and attention when their fathers are away at war. It gives me hope.

In my own journey toward spiritual fatherhood I have, at times, found myself questioning whether or not I had the heart to be a father in the natural or the spiritual realms. I, like many other fathers, feared that I wouldn't be a good parent. I had fears that I would repeat the mistakes of my family of origin. We have a family history filled with trouble between sons and fathers, as well as addictions and divorce. Becoming a father in the church was even scarier. I have had a few seasons in ministry when I wanted to quit, but one thing the world can't afford is fathers and mothers quitting in either the natural or spiritual realms. Nevertheless, I have stood on that precipice and looked over the edge a time or two. I would like to share a painful situation that led me to seek God's help, a situation in which God first renewed my heart and then turned it toward my spiritual children. Prior to this crisis I had thought I was able to lead and nurture people well. Coming up against this crucible showed me I wasn't.

In the story I am about to tell, Pam and I had formed a team for a new ministry and soon after went through the most difficult time we have ever experienced. My main point isn't who did what, but rather the overhaul God performed on my heart during the experience. I want to serve as an example of how our Heavenly Father clearly sees into our hearts, and lovingly works through difficult circumstances to correct those hearts. He will soften, renew, or even transplant the whole thing, if needed. His goal is to bring us to the point of choosing to obey Him because we trust Him. He really is serious about "turning our hearts."

It is hard to say when things began to fall apart between myself and a member of our team I shall call "Chris." I had noticed that Chris had seemed angry and distant on a few occasions, but this behavior wasn't uncommon as Chris, like many of us, seemed to be going through a lot of "pruning." One evening, though, during a leaders' meeting, Chris confronted me about my leadership. In front of our entire core team, Chris asked if I knew of anyone in the ministry that was following my leadership. Chris then turned to Pam and asked if *she* was following me. I was stunned and so were the other leaders.

If I had understood what was going on behind the scenes before, during, and after this confrontation, I would have responded a little differently than I did. That night I did the only thing I could think of — politely dismiss everyone after a closing prayer, and retreat to my basement. I quickly sent out an email to two trusted friends, told them what had just occurred, and asked them to pray for me so that I would have wisdom in my response. I then descended into a tailspin of depression that lasted about two weeks, telling all our team members to leave me alone during that time.

I didn't know the extent of my problem and if I had, I would have gone for help immediately instead of waiting. To be brief, Chris and others were maneuvering behind the scenes to remove me from the ministry. We had trusted them, and their betrayal and rejection of us were devastating. After several days, I finally scheduled a three-hour appointment at Elijah House with a counselor. I fully expected God to be sympathetic and to coddle me. Little did I know He was about to deal with heart issues that hindered my effectiveness as a father in the kingdom. As you can probably imagine, my issues were also a barrier between me and God, and He wasn't going to have any more of that, either!

When I arrived at Elijah House, I was depressed, and I struggled to tell my story to the counselor. He was quite patient and insightful. After getting enough detail, he looked at me and told me that it was time to ask God to show me what He wanted to do. As he prayed, I immediately went into a vision.

I saw myself wearing a multicolored robe, much like the one I imagined Joseph might have had. I had a staff in my right hand, and I was hunkered down behind this very large, dark object that looked like it might be a rock. I had just barely made these observations when I heard the voice of God. He said:

"Move back, I am going to remove your heart of stone and give you a new heart of flesh." (based on Ezekiel 36:26)

As I heard His voice, I looked up and saw a large hammer coming down out of heaven. It was moving toward the dark object (my heart) I just described to you. My thoughts were all over the place. I wondered if this was real. I wondered if I was far enough away from my heart to avoid getting hurt. Then I thought, "Oh man, if this is my heart then this is going to hurt anyway!" I certainly hadn't expected this from God. Where was the coddling and encouragement? This was downright bizarre. As the hammer came down, I felt no pain. I couldn't see what had happened to my heart, but I knew that He had done something important. I was then instructed by God to turn around. As I turned around, I saw a staircase illumined from a faint light glowing above. There appeared to be a doorway of some kind. The Voice then told me to go up the stairs. At this point, part of me wanted to laugh. I thought, "Who is going to believe this? I am being told by God to walk toward the light. This is so clichéd!" As I moved toward the first step, I felt a weight in my hand that was holding me back. I looked down and saw an old man. After wondering why I was dragging an old man around, I looked a little closer and was astonished to discover that the old man was me. As I struggled up the stairs, dragging my old man behind me, the vision ended.

When I began to sort this out with the counselor, I began to get the picture. I recognized that I had a few rules that I lived by, including this one: If I am nice to you, you should be nice to me. This rule was useful because it protected me from criticism and confrontation, and confrontation, with its attendant risks, had to be avoided because I was already dragging around a burden of unresolved guilt and shame from my old nature. My defensiveness and my burden made it difficult to be a spiritual father. I was so insecure that I was more interested in approval than in helping others face their own issues. During the remainder of the three-hour session, I spent some time repenting and forgiving, not realizing that the earlier scene at the leaders' meeting was only a preface. The whole story had yet to be revealed and dealt with. I didn't fully understand that I needed to be relieved of my hard heart and old ways. I would come to realize later that the experience that had led me to seek counseling was a merciful act of God. It was severe mercy, but mercy nonetheless.

After the session, I got into my car and headed home aware that God had done something significant with my heart. I knew it would take awhile to connect my heart and head, but this was a work of the Holy Spirit, and as such, I knew I could trust His ways, though I didn't really understand them. I was about to go home to deal with the trouble Chris and a few others had stirred up. With my new heart and new resolve, I hoped I would be able to navigate through the waves of adversity and pain, caring for God's children in a healthier way. We had a leader retreat coming up, and I knew that things would happen there that would either make me or break me as a leader. I needed God to turn my heart toward His children so I could stand on their behalf, while dealing bravely with the opposition that desired to remove me and gain control of our new ministry. I knew if I quit, the ministry would die or become extremely unhealthy. By focusing on how my actions would affect the young believers in our ministry, I kept my resolve to stand. I later understood that this difficult situation and my healing process were what God used to "turn my heart to His children." I was clearly more concerned about avoiding conflict and gaining approval.

Our retreat started as usual, with fun and games on a Thursday night, and a full agenda waiting for us on Friday morning. Early Friday morning, the Lord spoke to me. He told me there were people on our team downstairs who were seeking to remove me from the ministry, but they would first attempt to decrease my influence. He then told me to "stand up." I shared what God had said with Pam, and the two of us braced ourselves and headed downstairs. When we got into the meeting, I quickly realized that a small contingent had indeed been talking prior to the retreat and had determined they wanted me to step aside from my usual role in the ministry for a period of six months. They justified their position by citing my depression and claiming I was generally ineffective. The tension in the room was very high. I knew that if I capitulated, the ministry would fail, so I decided to obey God and "stand up." I had to trust Him and believe that He was with me.

Our ministry was headed for a split, and my silence wouldn't cut it anymore. I gently but firmly let the faction know that I would continue to do the ministry that God had given me to do. My statement brought a bitter, angry response, and it became painfully apparent that I needed to close down the morning session and to cancel the afternoon one, as well.

Pam and I went upstairs and I confided in her my desire to go home. She informed me that to do so would empower those in rebellion and therefore, we should stay. (I love my wife!) It would have been easy to run in the midst of betrayal and rejection, but a mature father stands firm. Because God had already begun my heart transformation, I recognized this immediately, so we stayed.

We managed to have some fun that evening playing cards and watching movies. Later, after we went to bed, the Lord reminded me of some lessons a spiritual father had once taught me. He had advised me to appoint people to the leadership team who were committed to me and to the vision that God had given me. He told me to make certain the people I pulled alongside me had the necessary character and maturity to remain trustworthy and faithful. He also warned me to be sure people were emotionally stable and secure enough to be leaders.

Next, the Lord told me that I was partly to blame for what was going on. That was hard to face. You see, I believe God had directed me to plant a pastor-led ministry, but I had decided to make it a board-run ministry instead. I had been afraid of rejection, so I headed it off at the pass by foolishly disobeying. As I lay in bed, I realized my course was wrong. I asked forgiveness from God that night and from the people involved at a later date. God then dropped the bomb: He told me that some of the leaders had been discussing my removal from the ministry altogether. I was to confront a particular man in the morning to confirm this. As you can imagine, I didn't sleep much that night.

The next morning, soon after loading the vans, I caught the attention of the man in question. I asked him to follow me around the corner of the house where I privately questioned him as the Lord had directed. "Have there been discussions about my removal from the ministry by you, Chris, or others?" He stammered and stuttered and finally blurted out "yes." Following a short discussion, I let him know that when we got home I would take a couple of days to decide how to handle this, and then we would meet again. Later that morning at breakfast, I wept bitterly. I had never felt that kind of pain before. The full weight of what was happening hit me like a ton of bricks. Pam and I had a mess on our hands. We were facing a split in the core team that could potentially divide the ministry.

My plan was simple. In a well crafted letter, we would ask those involved to step down as leaders and to get counseling with a stated goal of reconciliation after a season of rebuilding trust. I called in two other core team couples to help me with the letter, which we then sent off. Within 24 hours, a faithful member of the leadership team received a response to the letter and a meeting was set.

The meeting took less than ten minutes. I was informed that the leaders in question had heard from God and that it was His desire for them to leave. There would be no discussion and no counseling. This was effectively their last meeting with us. I had known ahead of time, in my spirit, this would occur, so I asked the people involved to write an appropriate resignation letter that could be read in front of everyone involved in the ministry, which they did.

When I read their letter at the close of the ministry meeting that week, I found that people were extremely supportive of Pam and I, and many were visibly relieved. Because God is always faithful, our losses were minimal, and the lessons I learned from God during this season have allowed me to continue in my growth as a father and leader in the kingdom. I am much more proactive as a spiritual father and leader than ever before. This experience has enabled me to be involved in the lives of people in a healthier way. I approach issues with people more readily and with less anxiety than before because I have grown in love and have more concern for the flock than for how circumstances might affect me. I no longer avoid the pain of confrontation, but embrace it knowing that we are to speak in love (Ephesians 4:15) for their good.

Getting that "heart transplant" was a necessary step in the spiritual training I have received from the Lord. It was His radical way of "turning my heart to the children." The Scripture quoted at the beginning of this chapter indicates that giving us a father's heart is God's agenda.

You may be surprised how He renews your heart, but He will collaborate with you if that is your desire. Heart renewal is a prerequisite to becoming a spiritual father to those God calls you to raise up in the kingdom. It is absolutely vital for you to have His heart for His people.

CHAPTER 3

Walking in the Father's Blessing

"Blessed are the poor in spirit,
For theirs is the kingdom of heaven.
Blessed are those who mourn,
For they shall be comforted.
Blessed are the meek,
For they shall inherit the earth.
Blessed are those who hunger and
thirst for righteousness,
For they shall be filled.
Blessed are the merciful,
For they shall obtain mercy.
Blessed are the pure in heart,
For they shall see God.
Blessed are the peacemakers,
For they shall be called sons of God.
Blessed are those who are persecuted
for righteousness sake,
For theirs is the kingdom of heaven."
Matthew 5:3-10

Character Formation

The eight "blessed" character qualities or attitudes listed above are probably familiar to most Christians who have been around for awhile. But a spiritual father can't settle for "familiar" here. For many years I failed to grasp how important it is that fathers experience each beatitude while they are in training.

Mature fathers attain these attributes through experience and growth challenges. Before God releases us into great blessing and fruitfulness, He has to spend time pruning us. He prunes our motives and our attitudes, and then He works us into alignment with His agenda.

In this chapter I want to lay a foundation for understanding the character traits God is looking to instill in each one of us. I hope that we manifest all eight of these attitudes in our lives because if we do, we will be blessed, and God will move through us.

Blessed Are the Poor in Spirit

To be poor in spirit defines a person who sees himself as totally and completely bankrupt spiritually. We have absolutely nothing to offer God but the life He gave us. Therefore, true happiness and contentment are only found at the cross. Only at the cross are we able to face the total depravity of our nature and yet know the two things spiritual children know: Our Daddy in heaven loves us, and our sins are forgiven! An immature person fails to see his abject spiritual poverty before God. When we fail to see ourselves as needy, we get the old "I can take care of myself" attitude. In our culture we are taught to have "pride" and to strike out and make it on our own. People who succeed and those who "arrive," are esteemed in our society. When we realize our poverty, our blindness, and our nakedness, then God's heart is moved. In God's economy, a "poverty spirit" of this kind attracts Him and His grace.

One of the most difficult things I personally faced when we planted our current church, Desert Rock Fellowship was my own neediness both spiritually and financially. I was just starting up my private practice as a counselor, and we had very little income. I didn't know how to do a lot of things that were required of a church planter and senior pastor because my experience had been limited to youth pastor and associate pastor. I didn't know the ways of God very well yet, either. The first charismatic church I ever attended on a regular basis was the one I was planting. Needless to say, my learning curve was very steep.

God allowed me to be broken and humbled by letting me see my own financial poverty. We had people walk up to us and give us money constantly during the church's first four years. I had never taken anything from anyone before that. We were given gifts that totaled over $45,000 during that four-year period. God's provision for our financial poverty was astounding. During times of spiritual poverty, my friend and mentor, Tom Miller, called me frequently. God always seemed to have Tom call when I was in a spiritual quandary. With counsel and prayer, I was able to cast aside all self-reliance and instead seek the constant grace of God. This process started with the Holy Spirit showing me my utter poverty apart from the cross.

Early in our ministry at Desert Rock, God reminded me of an experience I had had with Him when I was about 19 years old. I was sitting in my customary seat in church one Sunday morning, just sort of messing around with a friend during a communion service. As I was goofing off, we received the communion elements. I was holding the cup of grape juice when my hand jerked reflexively (think hammer on your knee). A small amount of the juice spilled onto my finger and thumb, and it looked like blood. I then heard the Lord say to me, "I died for you, too!" I was ashamed and humbled at the time, and I felt humbled again when He brought back the memory.

We are all needy and in great spiritual poverty apart from His provision and blessing. Walking with God in true humility will bring you His blessing. Remember, the Bible says, *"God resists the proud, but gives grace to the humble" (James 4:6b).*

Blessed Are Those Who Mourn

To mourn spiritually means to be filled with deep regret over your sin and the sinful state of the world. The mourner Jesus refers to understands the extent and the effect evil has in creation and has the capacity to mourn for himself, for his friend, and for his world. This capacity to mourn is compassionate in nature. Compassion will enable a father to mourn with others when they mourn (Romans 12:15), and those who mourn will be blessed according to our passage. The blessing they receive is to be comforted. For Isaiah the prophet, the favor of God came when the Messiah "preached good news to the poor, and brought them comfort" (Isaiah 61).

A couple of years ago, I was invited to lead one of the small groups at a "round table" event for leaders in our region. During this process, one of the men broke down and wept as he shared his grief over losing his father a few months earlier. He was overwhelmed with the burden of directing the vast ministry his dad had left behind. One of the other ministers, perhaps uncomfortable with the display, began trying to encourage the mourner with clichés such as "God promised to never leave or forsake us." I interrupted him and apologized to the man who was grieving. We then listened further, validated his pain, and with his permission invited the Holy Spirit to be a comfort to him through prayer, laying on of hands, and hugs. Some of us wept with him through the prayer. When we were finished, he shared that he had felt God's touch through us, and he thanked us because he was encouraged and strengthened by what we had done.

And what about the gentleman who tried to help? He learned something that day and expressed gratitude for it later. Though trying to be helpful, he had failed to embrace the emotional content of what the man in grief was sharing. To be able to grieve with another, avoid the common mistake of ignoring the emotional content of the mourner's message. If you bypass the emotional content to get to the intellectual issue, you effectively shut them down; they won't feel heard.

I spent an entire semester in seminary learning to listen, understand, and reflect back the intellectual and emotional content of the counselee's issues and pain. We learned how to validate the counselee's pain, whether it was logical and rational or not. When I first signed up for the class I thought it would be a waste of time, but it has proved to be a life saver. When you are in a situation with someone who is grieving, simply ask open ended questions like "What does that feel like to you?" or "What hurts the most?" Try to avoid questions that require "yes" or "no" answers. Sometimes you just need to sit in silence with them and possibly hold them, with their permission.

Connecting with another is done on three levels if it is to be effective. The rational content, emotional content, and spiritual issues all need to be touched. It is important for you to determine whether you are uncomfortable with the pain of another. If you do experience discomfort or suspect you may, ask the Lord to heal you and conform you to His image in this area. He will.

We are told in Galatians 6 that we are to bear one another's *burdens*. According to this passage everyone has a daily load they are responsible to carry. Working, taking care of ourselves, and meeting our family's physical needs fall into the *load* category. But everyone, whether family, friend, acquaintance, or stranger, will experience earth shattering and overwhelming events in life that bring grief. Without a heart of compassion, we will miss the opportunity to bear one another's burdens in a significant way.

Much of my ministry has been as a counselor. I have discovered that when you mourn with another, you find God. He always has an agenda to reveal Himself as He meets the needs of His loved ones. As you mourn with people, God releases His comfort to them through you. Compassion is really a work of grace that is activated by God's Spirit moving through our hearts.

41

As a conduit of His love during difficult times, you learn the heart of the Father for His people, and you are comforted yourself when your turn comes. Spiritual fathers and mothers are sought out in times of pain and turmoil. To be effective as such, we must embrace each person's pain and learn to bear their burdens. In doing so, we reflect Jesus' love and grace to them

.

Blessed Are the Meek

In God's economy the meek inherit the earth. I used to believe meekness equaled weakness. However, if you look carefully at this word in the Greek, you will find that it has more to do with high moral fiber, the ability to be strong and disciplined about your convictions, while being gentle, and humble. A meek person is able to obey God because of his humility. His acknowledged need of the cross gives him a healthy respect and fear of God.

We often mistake meekness for shyness, but these two qualities actually conflict. Allowing one's reclusive nature to interfere with the ability to carry a message that needs to be heard is in conflict with the strength of character that defines one who is meek. Having strength of character implies the ability and responsibility to speak up in faith. When a meek individual does so, the Holy Spirit brings the needed favor to bring changes to situations that cause righteous influence to reign. In this process the meek inherit the earth. Spiritual fathers will possess all the character qualities of meekness and will speak into situations and see this "inheritance."

It is impossible in the natural to assume a meek person would inherit or possess the earth. But with God, and against all odds, this will occur. I long to see this character trait manifest in fathers so that we can see His power and presence overcome and subdue the earth through us.

Blessed Are Those Who Hunger and Thirst for Righteousness

In a world where we wake up and turn on our tap to get water, and then proceed to rummage through our refrigerators and cupboards to choose from a variety of foods to eat for breakfast, this idea of being hungry and thirsty is pretty foreign. To be blessed, a spiritual father must constantly hunger for righteousness. He must long to live a life conforming to God's will. The promise of being filled comes to those in this state. The church is full of people who desire just a little bit of God, a little bit of religion, and a little bit of a little bit ... and some things they don't want at all. Mature fathers and mothers are radical in their pursuit of obedience and holiness. Some who follow hard after God are labeled as "religious" or "fanatical." Believe me when I say that these people have learned what causes the presence of God to abide with them and what chases Him away. Choose intimacy and holiness if you want to see His glory manifest in your life and ministry. Without them, you will lack both favor and blessing.

I have gone through seasons of being so hungry and thirsty that I was willing to pay thousands of dollars to get to meetings where I thought God might show up. My wife, Pam, and I went to Toronto several times just to get into His presence and to see the miracles He was doing there. We knew that if we were in His presence, then we would experience Him and be changed. We desired to be holy as He is holy. We couldn't get enough of Him and the change that came in our hearts due to seeing Him in His glory. It is time for the church to turn from our contrary ways and to seek to walk in purity again. We must do what we can to pursue Him and His will.

Blessed Are the Merciful

Merciful people are shown mercy. Mercy is defined as a compassionate "loving-kindness" that isn't so much emotional as it is intentional. The idea is to honor God for His mercy toward you by showing mercy to others. In the Scriptures we are told that we reap what we sow (Galatians 6:7-8). Those who are genuinely forgiven should reciprocate. Mature spiritual fathers know this well. I can't imagine having a spiritual father who wasn't merciful with my screw ups, although I must confess I've been chastised for a lack of mercy. Let me relate an experience in which I honestly believe I had the finger of God on my chest all night. Here's what happened.

Early in my ministry I was offended by a couple of local ministers. They had done some things that I thought were pretty underhanded, and I judged them as men who lacked character. After sharing my experiences with a pastor that I trusted, I was directed by him to talk to a couple of other men who had complaints about the same two gentlemen. (It is never a good idea to take advice from people who are as offended as you are!) We decided it would be a great idea to confront these guys. I ended up writing them a letter, and I alone signed it. Yes, if you haven't figured it out by now, I am not the sharpest tack in the box. I mailed the letter feeling pretty satisfied that I was God's messenger; I was very self-righteous about the whole thing. That night I went to bed and found that I couldn't sleep because I had a weight on my chest, an unshakable "holy fear." After hours of praying and listening, somewhere around 5:30 a.m., I heard the still, small voice of God. He said:

"I have shown thee, oh man, what is good; I told you to do justly, love mercy and walk humbly before Me. But you love justice!" (based on Micah 6:8)

Needless to say, I was dumbfounded at how stupid I had been, and I resolved to repent to the two men as soon as possible. Simply put, I had lacked mercy. I had been so offended, I failed to see that I didn't have God's heart for those two. Moses misrepresented the heart of God when he was angry and struck the

44

rock (Numbers 20:11), and he never made it into the promised land.

There is a lesson in here for all of us, isn't there? Do not go to bed in your anger (Ephesians 4:26); forgive, and then humbly deal with your neighbor. When I awoke I called one of my elders and had him set up a breakfast meeting with the two ministers. I instructed him to kick me really hard underneath the table if I started pursuing an argument that would force the ministers to see things my way. In the meeting, I apologized (gee whiz, that's hard when you are the one who's right). I learned that we didn't see things in the same way, and that we had to agree to disagree agreeably. It was about seven or eight years later that I got some closure in a discussion with one of them. Isn't God good? Mercy is good. Let's get some and give a ton of it away.

Blessed Are the Pure in Heart

This beatitude is one of my favorites. To be pure in heart is to have an undivided integrity in your heart. Purity of heart can be described as having wholeness, without division, as to motives and intentions in pleasing God. In our culture, it is common for people to have "moral schizophrenia" due to our penchant for acting out on our evil impulses. Having a divided heart is the opposite of having a pure heart. We cannot be of two minds and be pure.

I shared earlier in the "Honoring Fathers" section of the book that I had met Denny Cline when several prophets had come to our place to conduct a conference and that Denny had invited a few of us to join them. The first night a young prophet spoke about how the "pure in heart would see God." As I sat there, I couldn't shake the obvious question, "Did I have a pure heart?" I asked the Lord several times and heard nothing but silence. I finally figured that He must think my heart was pure or He would tell me differently. About a week or two after the conference, I was up in Spokane at my favorite retreat location spending a couple of days trying to hear from God. One night I awoke from an incredible dream.

In the dream, I was playing pinochle with one of my best friends, Martin, and his dad, Stuart, and an unknown person whose face I couldn't see. I was dealt 5 eights, and I way overbid my hand. It was a little terrifying because Martin couldn't help me, and the "unknown" person was now up in heaven arguing with God about my fate. I heard some things about my epitaph being spoken between the two, but I couldn't get a clear picture on what the decision was going to be.

When I awoke, I must have spent 15 to 20 minutes trying to hear an interpretation of the dream. I finally heard God ask me, "What did you have in your hand?" I puzzled about that for a moment because I had had 5 eights, and pinochle decks don't have eights. Then it hit me like a ton of bricks. The 5 eights symbolized Matthew 5:8. ("Blessed are the pure in heart for they will see God.") I found myself crying in the dark with a joy that I couldn't describe in a million years. I would see God — I held the confirmation in my hand!

If a father in the kingdom fails to have a pure heart, he will not know the way of freedom and won't be effective at helping others get free. One more tidbit, just because you or I have a pure heart today, doesn't mean we can't have an impure heart tomorrow. A pure heart stays pure by a washing with the blood through consistent confession of our sins and by avoiding evil that taints and darkens us. The pure in heart are blessed. Spiritual fathers know this.

Blessed Are the Peacemakers

Peacemakers "seek peace and pursue it" (Psalm 34:14). Peacemaking isn't passive acceptance of whatever comes along. I became a peace*keeper* early in life. This is different from being a peace*maker*. True peacemakers always desire God's best for those they serve. They have an active involvement that confronts the problem effectively. Only mature spiritual fathers have the skill sets needed to bring reconciliation in difficult situations. It takes good conflict resolution skills and mature relational skills to bring healing to hard places.

Speaking of hard places, when I was in my early thirties, I had a nearly impossible job. My task was to implement and manage student assistance programs in 23 school districts in a six-county region in southeast Washington. I was working with principals and counselors to get a program in place that would educate staff on how to identify drug- and alcohol-addicted students, and to get them to treatment or sobriety groups during school hours on campus. I also had to hire, train, and oversee intervention specialists who would set up groups dealing with anger management, children of alcoholics, and students who were currently drinking and using. I had responsibilities to write curriculum for the intervention specialists to use in the groups and for teachers to use in the classroom. In my spare time, I found myself counseling teachers, principals, and school counselors who were having problems with students and their peers. I was working about 70 hours a week and missed my wife and children. One night after a few months on the job, I was driving home and in my frustration said out loud, "What am I doing out here?" I immediately heard the voice of the Lord say, "Blessed are the peacemakers." I was shocked. I had never thought of myself as a peacemaker. I realized that the man who had hired me chose me out of a pool of over 50 candidates, most of whom were younger and less experienced than I. I have never forgotten, that as believers, we are all called to be peacemakers in the kingdom.

My personal belief is that fathers in the kingdom are the ones who do this well most often. Children and young men often lack the incumbent wisdom and experience to triumphantly wrestle with difficult issues. Because of this they often lack the trust and favor of others as well. It is good for them to seek the wisdom of fathers to help them fulfill the mandate of being peacemakers. We must remember that peacemakers are blessed by God.

We will deal with the final beatitude, which concerns persecution, in the fifth chapter when we discuss tactics young men need to learn to become fathers who overcome. At this point you may be wondering why I chose to begin this chapter with the beatitudes instead of 1 Timothy 3. Although 1 Timothy deals with behavior and reputation, which are important, the beatitudes deal with the *heart* of a man. The Lord has taught me much about the beatitudes and their place in the character and lives of spiritual fathers. Remember, in order to become a fruitful and mature spiritual father, God needs to deal with your heart.

Part Two

What Spiritual Young Men Learn: Spiritual Discernment, Application of the Word, and How to Overcome Their Enemies

Chapter 4

Acquiring Wisdom and Discernment

"Do not quench the Spirit. Do not despise prophecies.
Test all things; hold fast to what is good. Abstain
from every form of evil."
1 Thessalonians 5:19-22

Learning to Hear God's Voice

Have you ever heard God call your name? Some of you are answering "no" too quickly! This isn't a trick question either! If you are born again, you have heard His voice call your name. It may not have been a physically audible encounter like some of the biblical characters had, but your spirit has heard Him nonetheless. The Holy Spirit woos us and brings us into a place of decision as He works to introduce us to Jesus and the Father. Once we understand the gospel and accept Jesus as Savior and Lord, and once we read the gospels, we find out that we all hear His voice (John 10:27).

I remember the first time I became aware that God was talking to me beyond wooing me into a relationship with Him. I had been saved at age five and knew then that He had pursued me. But this situation was different. I was a 12 year old in junior high at the time. I had just left school and was headed toward a trail in the woods that many of us took as a shortcut on the way home. As I got to the base of the trail, I had an overwhelming sense that there was danger ahead. I tried to ignore it, but couldn't. I quietly walked up the trail and peered around a bend to discover that two "bad kids" were up ahead, and I knew they didn't like me much. I knew I could whip the one, but I also knew that the other one could probably clean my clock, and both of them together would completely overwhelm me. I realized that it was God who was warning me, so I turned around and went home a different way. The next day my sister heard from some mutual friends that the two boys had hatched a plan to jump me on that trail and wondered why they hadn't seen me.

It's tragic that so many of us don't think that God has ever called our name. A large percentage of the Christians I meet in America believe that just having the Scriptures is enough. They have no expectation of having revelation and interaction with the Holy Spirit beyond "feeling the conviction of sin." It isn't surprising to me because I was the same way for years. Part of the problem has to do with what is commonly taught in some evangelical seminaries.

In my own experience, I was taught that once the canon of Scripture was completed, all "sign gifts" ceased. This doctrine is part of what is known as dispensational theology. The essence of this dogma is that God chose to reveal His kingdom in the way He did for the early formation of the church, but once this occurred there was no longer a need for the sign gifts, and those gifts eventually ceased. Dispensational theology is a way of describing different stages in the progression of revelation that God has given while working out His will over time.

The gifts in question are tongues, interpretation of tongues, prophecy, healing, and miracles. These gifts are seen as unnecessary or as having ceased in dispensational theology. Yet the gifts of teaching, pastoring, service, and hospitality (along with a few others) are still valued. My point is that this doctrine has contributed greatly to our lack of intimacy with God and has interfered with the body of Christ even seeking to hear His voice. Spiritual deafness in turn is a major reason that so many lack discernment. Learning to hear God's voice is a necessary step toward gaining discernment. A young man needs to develop wisdom and discernment before becoming a spiritual father, because decision making, counseling, and disciplining all require discernment.

It is easy to understand why so few Christians possess the sign gifts, when you realize that this particular point of dispensational dogma is commonly taught in seminaries and Bible schools. Once pastors are trained to deny these gifts, they pass on their "knowledge" to the church. Dispensational theology, or at least the portion that denies the existence of certain gifts, is in direct conflict with the Scriptures recorded for you at the opening of this chapter. The promoters of this dogma get around obeying those particular verses by using a strange interpretation of 1 Corinthians 13:8-10, which supposedly makes these gifts obsolete to the church:

"Love never fails. But whether there are prophecies, they will fail; whether there are tongues, they will cease; whether there is knowledge, it will vanish away. For we know in part and we prophesy in part. But when that which is perfect has come, then that which is in part will be done away."

They teach that "the perfect" has come in the form of the completion of the Scriptures. The inspired word of God was completed near the end of the first century. But the need for the gifts and their power has not ceased. In 1 Corinthians 14:1, the Bible tells us to:

"Pursue love, and desire spiritual gifts, but especially that you may prophesy."

The word translated "desire" is *zeloo* in the Greek, which means "to be zealous for, to burn with desire, to pursue ardently, to desire eagerly or intensely" (Strong's #2206). Why would God tell us to lust after this gift if we wouldn't need it up until the time

Jesus returns? Jesus is "the perfect" who is coming. He will return at the completion of God's purposes in the last "dispensation." That is what the passage is really telling us.

Following a friendly debate with a fellow pastor, he told me that he "would rather have his can of worms than my can of worms." He was referring to his being in a church where they disallowed the sign gifts and comparing it with mine where we actively seek the manifest presence of God. I told him that to be in obedience with God's Word he doesn't have that option. That ended the debate, and fortunately, the friendship was spared.

You may wonder why people would deny gifts at all, especially when they are found in Scripture. I will tell you from experience that the misuse of God's gifts by the immature and wounded has caused a great deal of fear among those who have been manipulated and spiritually abused in unhealthy Spirit-filled churches. Others have been put off by what they consider to be the "emotional excesses" they have seen in some Pentecostal services. Still, others like me had no reason to believe that the gifts in question were necessary, since we had always done church without them.

Unfortunately, some of the excuses for denying the gifts I have mentioned carry a lot of emotional weight for people when they decide "how and where they want their religion." Throwing the baby out with the bathwater is tragic, and that is what has happened with some concerning important and needed gifts that God gave the church. Many have decided to deny the "messy gifts" because they "cause so much trouble." In Luke 11:9-13, we find a challenge to the fear that so many wrestle with:

"So I say to you, ask, and it will be given to you; seek, and you will find; knock, and it will be opened to you. For everyone who asks receives, and he who seeks finds, and to him who knocks it will be opened. If a son asks for bread from any father among you, will he give him a stone? Or if he asks for a fish, will he give him a

serpent instead of a fish? Or if he asks for an egg, will he offer him a scorpion? If you then, being evil, know how to give good gifts to your children, how much more will your heavenly Father give the Holy Spirit to those who ask Him?"

While I was sharing some of my revelatory experiences with a brother, he confided in me that he was concerned that he might be deceived if he sought after the Holy Spirit and the gifts. I shared the above verse with him and with his permission, gently pushed back on his argument. I told him that it appeared to me he had more faith in the devil's ability to fool him than in God's ability to be true to His word. This made him laugh when he thought it through. He agreed with me, and we wondered how he had landed where he was with this whole issue.

When denying the existence of the sign gifts or any gift for that matter, we fail to honor God's Word. Beyond that, we disable ourselves. How? Without them, we are literally trying to do the work of the kingdom without all of the power and revelation available to us. This restriction limits our ability to perform our mission effectively, and we deny ourselves insight into God and the way He works. This diminishes our ability to be intimate with Him.

Recently, I have been preaching through the book of Ephesians and have rediscovered some truth I want to share here. In Ephesians 4:11-13 we are told:

"And He Himself gave some to be apostles, some prophets, some evangelists, and some pastors and teachers, for the equipping of the saints for the work of ministry, for the edifying of the body of Christ, till we all come to the unity of the faith and of the knowledge of the Son of God, to a perfect man, to the measure of the stature of the fullness of Christ."

Can any say, with a straight face, that His church has measured up to these verses? Then it stands to reason that the listed gifts are still essential, aren't they? All of God's gifts are love gifts and originate in the Holy Spirit. When a gift is given, it begins to manifest and grow in you if you nurture it. It blooms best when you acquire God's heart for the lost and broken. When you begin to activate the gift of prophecy, you begin to see with "His eyes" and to hear with "His ears." You will begin to feel with His heart and to act with His agenda in mind. When you operate in the gift of healing, you will begin to understand God's power and compassion at a different level. When you see how He manifests in various ministry situations, you will appreciate and understand His ways better. In that sense, you will grow up into Him.

As an example, while ministering in the Philippines recently with my friend, Duane Smith, we trained 291 pastors and Bible school students. After finishing the pastors' conference, we held a two-night crusade in a village nearby. The first night of the healing crusade Duane preached the gospel, and I taught the healing portion of the service. When Duane gave the altar call, quite a few came forward, but I noticed there were many "tougher" villagers outside the fenced area of the arena where the meetings were being held. The Holy Spirit gave me insight into what Duane needed to do so that they, too, could come into relationship with Jesus. I encouraged him to look beyond the fenced area to specifically invite those outside the arena to come in and receive Christ. As Duane did this, there seemed to be some reluctance from the villagers to come forward. Again the Holy Spirit prompted me to have Duane call out to them directly. As he did, one person came forward, then two more, and soon a stream of them were filing into the arena to receive Jesus as Savior and Lord. It was all very exciting. I believe more villagers who stood outside the arena were saved than those who had been seated inside.

After praying with the new converts, it was my turn to step forward and teach on healing. I first shared some stories from the Scriptures. Then I asked the people to come forward and receive their healing. That night we were disappointed that there were only three claiming to have been healed. A hip, a back, and a cough. I was bummed. I even went so far as to tell Duane if that was all that God was going to do in the healing realm, I wasn't sure I wanted to come back for the last night.

The next day I was still frustrated and complaining in my heart to the Lord when the Holy Spirit directed me to look up Luke 4:40. Here is what I found:

"When the sun was setting, all those who had any that were sick with various diseases brought them to Him; and He laid His hands on every one of them and healed them."

Was God asking me to leave the stage and lay hands on each individual? I was a little apprehensive of this idea for two reasons. First, it is important for people to know that it is *Jesus* who heals — not us. Often the people in remote areas of third world nations are not well educated and some may mistakenly believe we possess some sort of power originating in us. To combat this belief, we ask people to lay their own hands over the areas of their bodies that need healing and have them ask Jesus to heal them. That way they are praying directly to Jesus in faith (we hope!). We want them to realize that when they or someone they know needs healing in the future, they can simply ask Jesus.

The second reason I was hesitant to leave the stage is that it can be dangerous to do so. During the crusade, a Philippine FBI agent was assigned to us as our bodyguard. Similarly, while ministering in India, as many as 12 bodyguards were delegated to us, depending on where we were going, and how dangerous our hosts thought it might be.

After reading and pondering Luke 4:40, I asked the Lord if we were to lay hands on the people. He said "yes," but first we needed to ask permission of our hosts. I shared this with Pastor Bonifer, and after thinking a moment about it, he agreed. We then invited him, and a few of the pastors there with him, to join us and act as translators for us. I was excited to get to the meeting that night.

I never want to rush Duane through the gospel because he is so good at it, and salvation is important, but that night I was so excited about what might occur I was relieved when the altar call and prayer concluded. As I stepped forward to share, I knew in my spirit that this was going to be special. My flesh, on the other hand, was dreading the possibility of another slow night. After I called people forward to be healed, we quickly left the stage and began to lay hands on them. One after another, villagers began to run up the stairs and testify as God caused large goiters to fall off peoples' necks, backs were healed, and arthritis was healed. One woman in her late seventies told me through the translator that her back was severely curved and that she had debilitating rheumatoid arthritis throughout her back, hips, and legs. She was slightly hunched over, and from what I was told, had been watching the meeting from outside the arena. She brought her 30-year-old granddaughter with her because she suffered from the same curvature of the spine and from what I perceived was tuberculosis, as well.

As I told the translator to communicate to her that Jesus wanted to heal her, the heat in my left palm became very intense. I told her to ask Jesus to heal her, and then I would put my hand on her head, and she would be healed. She did as I asked and instantly she stood erect and began dancing circles around me. She immediately grabbed her granddaughter by the hand and asked the interpreter if I would "do her too?" The translator and I laughed about that, then repeated to the granddaughter the words we had spoken to her grandmother. When she asked Jesus to heal her, I placed my hand on her head, and she began to smile very broadly and speak very quickly while giggling intermittently. The interpreter started smiling and laughing, too. I had felt the heat in my palm when she prayed, and when I placed my hand on her head, it seemed to me that it was very intense. I asked the interpreter what she said. He laughed and then told me that she reported "feeling heat surge" through her whole body, that her back was healed, and her cough was gone. She was surprised by the whole encounter. When I asked him what was so funny, he chuckled and told me that she had asked if I could come back next year just in case they needed me.

I learned so much about the love of God that night. He wanted to touch the people, and we were His instruments. When you encounter His power in this way, you gain insight through experience, not just from words on a page, and you know Him better. For example, if I read everything that was written about Princess Diana I still wouldn't know her unless I had been able to spend time with her and experience her firsthand (when she was alive). It is the same for Christians who spend years reading the Bible, but never walk in the anointing and giftings of God.

So in reality, we are not called to seek the gifts just for the sake of having them to "carry out" ministry. In reality, we are really seeking the Lord Himself. You must have the full compliment of gifting that God has designed for you if you are to walk out your destiny and calling in full measure.

Very few people, if any, have all the gifts, so being tied into the body and learning to work as a team is important, too. Every individual needs to learn to hear God's voice and operate in some wisdom and discernment. My personal belief is that the gift of discernment of spirits is necessary for every believer who goes on the front lines in the kingdom. In fact, I believe the gift of discernment of spirits and the ability to wisely discern how to deal with situations are two necessary attributes for a spiritual father.

The gift of discernment of spirits is found in 1 Corinthians 2:10. It is the ability to discern the spirit world and detect whether a person is influenced by darkness or God. There are numerous biblical examples of men and women who were able to discern the enemy's plans and overcome them. Nehemiah was one of them. In Nehemiah 6 we find that he was faced with a band of evil men trying to intimidate him away from his task. He determined to trust God and to fulfill his mission. Nehemiah correctly discerned his enemy's strategy and intentions and refused to fall into his snare.

Young men in the faith need to learn to operate in this gift before they move on into fathering others. Discernment is a wonderful gift when it operates in love along with grace and faith. When you move in this gift, you are able to flow along in agreement with God's governmental authority. This gift allows us to make decisions based on God's truth and not on our own opinions or the opinions of others.

The Bible teaches that it is necessary to "discern" (1 Thessalonians 5:21-22). An incident occurred several years ago that could have altered my future and the future of several others if I had allowed myself to be intimidated from the course that God had set. My wife and I had heard that God was moving in Toronto, so we wanted to go and see for ourselves. Also, we had a friend in dire need of deliverance, but God chose not to finish the process through us for reasons only He understands. We felt led to take him along with us to see what God might do in Toronto. I knew this decision was right and God confirmed it for us. We didn't initially have the finances for the trip, so my wife Pam and I prayed about it. Within a few days she received some inheritance money, so we purchased our tickets and made arrangements for our accommodations. Although we were certain that this was God's plan, I felt there would be opposition to it.

Have you ever felt like you have had a *déjà vu* experience? I actually don't believe in *déjà vu* at all. The Bible tells us in Job 33:14-16:

"For God may speak one way, or in another, yet man does not perceive it. In a dream, in a vision of the night, when deep sleep falls upon men, while slumbering on their beds, then He opens the ears of men, and seals their instruction."

Before I came to understand these verses, I thought I was having *déjà vu* when a man came to my office to convince me to stay away from Toronto. As I sat staring at the man who wanted us to forego this trip, a flood of revelation whipped through my mind. I had evidently had a vision while I slept that God was bringing to memory, right when I needed it. I had experienced this conversation before and knew exactly what I was going to say to him to end it! I patiently listened as he tried to persuade me that if I went I would be deceived and my job would be in jeopardy. I let him finish, then kindly replied that he was entitled to his opinion but really had no authority to dictate where I spend my vacation time. Beyond that, he didn't have accurate information about what was going on in Toronto. He had not personally visited Toronto, but had been influenced by a group of naysayers on the internet, none of whom he knew. I informed him that I had talked with people who had actually attended services in Toronto and that I would be going in spite of his wishes. I let him know that I respected him, but in this case, disagreed with him. He got up and stormed out of my office, and I sat there stunned and happy! In the end, we did visit Toronto; our friend experienced a massive deliverance and is doing well to this day!

In this example, I had received revelation and had the discernment to apply it at the appropriate time in an appropriate way. In 1 Corinthians 8:1, we are told that "knowledge puffs up," so discernment and humility must go hand in hand. I could have told the gentleman in my office about the vision that God had used to warn me of him and further alienated him, but God in His mercy gave the revelation while I slept and made me aware of it only when it was needed. If God had given me awareness earlier, I may have become prideful and lacked love in how I dealt with him. Ultimately, love must be our motivation. First Corinthians 8:2-3 states:

"And if anyone thinks that he knows anything, he knows nothing yet as he ought to know. But if anyone loves God, this one is known by Him."

Love always builds up. Loving others must be our motivation and our plumb line to keep us true to God's will and His way as we exercise the gift of discernment and revelation. We must be careful not to harm people. Our motives will reveal if our discernment is counterfeit or the real deal. Discernment is about hearing God's voice in a moment and responding with humility, love, and obedience. Discernment isn't fear, mistrust, suspicion, condemnation, or man's opinion. Fear is actually a stumbling block to hearing God clearly. First John 4:18 says:

"There is no fear in love. But perfect love drives out fear because fear has to do with punishment. The one who fears is not made perfect in love."

It is apparent that discernment and maturity go hand in hand. If we are mature we will have discernment and not "be infants, tossed back and forth by the waves and blown here and there . . ." (Ephesians 4). The Bible teaches that young children lack discernment (Deuteronomy 1:39).

When seeking to gain maturity in discernment, I ask the Holy Spirit to help me make a distinction between His voice and my own mind, will, and emotions. Going back to the Toronto trip, it would have been easy for me to condemn my brother as being from the devil when he came to dissuade me from going. In my flesh I wrestled (briefly) with wanting to give him some slap therapy! But in His perfect will, God gave me revelation that allowed me to overcome a scheme of the devil, while preserving the relationship.

The Bible teaches us that to lack discernment is to lack sound judgment (Proverbs 6:32). We gain discernment through the renewing of our minds (Romans 12:2). To grow in discernment, ask God to reveal any darkness or deceit in your life so you can repent and have your mind renewed. When our minds are renewed, we are able to understand the times and the seasons and will see through facades and directly into the heart of a matter.

Mature, loving discernment helps us recognize good and evil, and it helps us recognize God's will in any situation we come up against. Discernment makes us wise. Ultimately, discernment is not about instinct, intuition, or a game of hit and miss. God's truth hits the mark every time!

I have a story to share with you that I hope will cement what I am conveying to you about discernment. I had been at a pastor friend's church for a special meeting with a visiting evangelist. The meeting was terrific and several of us were invited forward to receive prayer. During the prayer, the power of God hit me and I lay on the floor for quite some time. When I was finally able to get up, I noticed a commotion to my left about 30 feet away. Two or three people were attempting to cast out demons from a man who was down on all fours. The demons were mocking and growling, and I was immediately angered at the display.

I had a fair amount of deliverance ministry experience in my past and decided to help my friends. Immediately discerning that the strongman was hiding behind lesser demons, I began casting them out when the man suddenly jumped up and grabbed me around my collar. We promptly wrestled him back down to the ground and resumed dealing with this nasty demon. I became aware that my pastor friend was in the pew observing this situation as was a small crowd that had gathered. I was ready for some help. My friend moved forward, and grabbing the man's face, demanded the demon be silent and allow the man to speak. The man's eyes rolled around and then returned to normalcy. To my amazement, my friend then asked him if he wanted to be delivered. It never occurred to me that a person would *not* want deliverance. After what seemed like a very long, silent period, the man said "yes." My friend bound the spirit and it was over, or so I thought.

I watched the man run a few laps around the auditorium praising God, but in my spirit felt something still wasn't right. I detected the same discernment in the eyes of several others as well.

We all realized he wasn't totally delivered because the celebration felt like the same mocking spirit we had just witnessed. As people gathered their things to go home, I had a conversation with the pastor and some of the people who had stayed to help and watch. I found out that this particular man had been causing problems in the church for over 20 years. The pastor and the evangelist had cast some spirits out of him earlier that evening when I was out on the floor. They were able to help take him just so far in his deliverance. They had the discernment to see that he wasn't really sincere. I didn't.

On the way home I asked the Lord why the possessed man had been able to grab me. In my experience in deliverance ministry, no one had ever laid a hand on me in any manner, let alone violently. I felt the Holy Spirit instruct me that the man was cooperating with the demons, and he liked the attention. I also came to understand that my anger got in the way of my discernment. I had been offended by the way the demon was mocking God and my friends and, therefore, was at least partially operating in the flesh. Oops. It was a very humbling evening. I hope you will benefit from my lesson.

In this chapter, I have argued that learning to hear God's voice is an essential step in the process of growing from a young man into a father in the kingdom. When a young man learns to hear God's voice, he is able to exercise wisdom and discernment, which are necessary to give counsel, to make good decisions, and to discipline others. This truth should lead a young man to embrace all the gifts of the Spirit because he knows that they are required for kingdom work. In cooperating with God to use these gifts, he grows in intimacy with God because he experiences the power of God, and learns the character and heart of God. These are some of the things that fathers do. Now let's move on to examine how having discernment can affect a young believer's ability to emerge as an overcomer.

Chapter 5

Overcoming Persecution, Abuse, and Fear

"For I think that God has displayed us, the apostles,
last, as men condemned to death; for we have been made a
spectacle to the world, both to angels and to men. We are
fools for Christ's sake, but you are wise in Christ! We are
weak, but you are strong! You are distinguished, but we
are dishonored.
To the present hour we both hunger and thirst, and we
are poorly clothed, and beaten, and homeless. And we labor,
working with our own hands. Being reviled, we bless; being
persecuted, we endure; being defamed, we entreat. We have
been made as the filth of the world, the offscouring of all
things until now.
I do not write these things to shame you, but as my beloved
children I warn you. For though you might have ten thousand
instructors in Christ, yet you do not have many fathers; for in
Christ Jesus I have begotten you through the gospel.
Therefore I urge you, imitate me."

1 Corinthians 4:9-16

Dealing with Offense

The final beatitude that I promised to discuss in this chapter
is about dealing with persecution. The passage of Scripture above

is intended to show us an attitude that spiritual fathers possess that puts fathering into perspective. Our attitudes and outlook in life will determine how much we overcome and accomplish. It is readily apparent, when you read what Paul had to say, that our Christian walk isn't about our convenience. Persecution is always going to be a part of the life of a man or woman who walks in Christ's authority and character. One secret to overcoming persecution is to be fearless (Hebrews 13:6). I am learning the importance of this truth more and more as I progress in my walk with God and in my dealings with people. As I mentioned earlier in this book, like many of you, I have had a lot of painful encounters in my lifetime. I didn't handle all of them the way I am going to encourage you to. I don't think I am alone when I say I learn lessons best when I fail.

One of the first things a mature father needs to learn is what attitude to take when persecution comes. A mature father must choose to guard his heart and refuse to become offended. Persecution can lead to offense and offense can only occur when you are self-focused and prideful. A mature spiritual father is human and will likely experience anger at injustices and persecution. There is a normal grieving process that each of us goes through when we have pain and loss, whether it is the loss of a loved one or our reputations. If we have proper attitudes about ourselves and reasonable expectations concerning the plight of any believer who seeks to promote God's kingdom, persecution will not lead us to become offended.

As I mentioned earlier, I have been involved in several church plants and have traveled a fair amount. Quite a few years ago, I went through a very difficult season while being prepared by God to move on in my destiny and calling. As I was transitioning out of one location and into another, I was falsely accused of being an "Absalom" and a "false prophet" by two men who didn't know me well. About nine months later one of my accusers apologized in a happenstance meeting. I thought I had forgiven him, but I hadn't. I will relate the rest of this story after I share some insights I have learned about dealing with offense.

When evil things happen to us, we are quite often offended. Offense is like a systemic poison that pollutes everything. As in high school chemistry, let one drop of ink fall into a beaker of pure water and all the water in the beaker becomes discolored. Offense is like that ink or like the leaven in bread. The beaker of water is totally affected, and so is the whole loaf of bread.

When you are hurt and offended, you will go through a process of experiencing first the surprise of being harmed, then anger, and soon after (hopefully) you will begin to find God's agenda and perspective of the offending person. You will know you are on the way to forgiving and canceling his debt when you are willing to ask God for direction and you seek to gently confront the offender. During a loving confrontation, explain how you were hurt in hopes that the offender will own what he did, and ask forgiveness from you, which will allow you both to move on and rebuild trust. Unfortunately, it doesn't always work out that cleanly, and here is why.

If you take a careful look through the Psalms and Proverbs, you will see three types of individuals that you need to identify if you are to keep yourself from unnecessary trouble. The first type of individual is the run-of-the-mill, ordinary man like you and me. Psalms and Proverbs refer to these folks as your friend or your neighbor. Both books talk about our frailty and need for grace and forgiveness. Jesus told us that we need to forgive seventy times seven (Matthew 18:22). So when one of your friends or neighbors sins against you, walk through the process described above.

The second type of person described in the Psalms and Proverbs is the "fool." When a fool sins against you, you still need to go through the process of forgiving them and even the process of the loving confrontation. But realize that they may not own what they did. The descriptions of a fool are not very flattering.

They are like dogs who return to their own vomit (Proverbs 26:11). They repeat the same errors over and over again. Wisdom says you limit your time around these people (Proverbs 13:20). Fools have hardened their hearts toward the ways of God and wisdom. Therefore, you need to be wise in how much time you spend with them, even if they are extended family members.

The third type of person you find described in the Psalms and Proverbs is the "wicked" or "evil" man. They lay snares for you (Psalm 119:110) and are deceivers who seek to take advantage of you (Proverbs 11:18). The Scriptures tell us to completely stay clear of these people. Our prisons are full of these folks. Many of them have personality disorders and seared consciences. Forgiving them is a must, but having any ongoing relationship with them isn't wise. (Some are called to work with this type of person, and we need to bless them for it. I have a few in my current church who have prison ministries, and I applaud them. I, too, worked with this population when I was employed in a psychiatric hospital. God is big enough to apply the healing power of the cross to anyone.) Don't allow guilt or manipulation by men to keep you in relationships that are destructive. Allow the Holy Spirit to define all your relationships, and you will do well.

Along with the "ordinary" sinners, the "fools," and the "evil ones," the church body also includes those we could describe as Jezebels, people who in fact cause great trouble in the church. Scripture instructs us to remove Jezebels from the flock (Jude 19), hopefully in a manner that is loving, wise, and firm. While doing so, we must also offer (and pay for) counseling toward their healing. The spiritual authority in such situations must guard against taking action out of offense and fear, treating the Jezebel as though he is hopeless and hopelessly condemned by God. To do so would be a form of spiritual abuse.

Let me here briefly define spiritual abuse. Spiritual abuse occurs when someone in authority uses their position to control, dominate, or manipulate those under them. Whenever a leader mistreats those in need of help, and the effect is further damage rather than healing, spiritual abuse has taken place. However, abuse does NOT occur simply because a spiritual authority disagrees with you and tells you "no." That is called leadership. (Please understand the difference.)

As a leader and as a spiritual father, you will be in tough situations dealing with difficult people. Count on it. In both positions, you must seek the highest degree of honesty and integrity to avoid what I call "reframing reality." In an occasion of spiritual abuse, a leader will ultimately manipulate an issue or problem by reframing it to rationalize and expedite a desired, often self-serving, course of action. Although it is true that a presenting problem is commonly a symptom of a greater, yet undiscovered problem, you'll want to lead in a way that is submitted to God because He is the giver of revelation, He knows our anxieties within us, He will try us and show us our wicked ways. Keep in mind that Psalm 85:10 tells us that mercy and truth are met together.

Now I want to get back to my story. I told you that I thought I had forgiven the men who had falsely accused me, but I hadn't. Here's what happened. When the men I was dealing with accused me of being an "Absalom" and a "false prophet," they were wrong. They crossed lines that displeased God. I was persecuted to the point of being spiritually abused. In my situation I was stuck between a rock and a hard spot. I was convinced that God wanted to do some new things where I ministered and that it would require us, as leaders, to get in front and pastor it. I saw the need to begin to be more open to the Holy Spirit, and unfortunately, this was a great threat. So some of those in authority decided that the issue wasn't what I said it was. They reframed the issue and told me that I was rebellious and had an agenda that would split and divide the church. It was then that the labels of "Absalom" and "false prophet" were given to me.

I knew the men didn't realize what they were doing. That means they weren't evil men, though they spoke evil. It doesn't even necessarily mean they were foolish men, though I believe they were offended and their hearts were hard. I believe they were my brothers and neighbors. The situation was terribly complex and basically I knew we needed a time apart to bring God's perspective. Once the key person apologized to me, I thought it was over. But it wasn't.

About a year or so after the apology, I realized through the nudges of the Holy Spirit that there were other men involved with the sin against me that I hadn't confronted. I needed to. I hated it, because in all honesty I didn't trust or respect them. Instead, I feared them. This was a problem; it was my problem. Under compulsion of the Holy Spirit I wrote out what had happened the year before from my perspective, and I defined spiritual abuse in the letter as I was certain they had been abusive toward me. It was a tearful and painful process that was both draining and healing. When I finished, I hoped that I wouldn't have to deliver it. But I couldn't shake the Holy Spirit's conviction that He was in this and wanted me to give the account to a particular man who was trustworthy.

I remember bringing the letter over to his house and being relieved he wasn't home. It was his day off, and I knew he could be anywhere. As I drove away, the Lord told me exactly where he was and directed me to deliver the letter to him. He was to give it to the others involved. I will never forget driving into this particular parking lot and behold — there he was, just like the Lord told me. He was simply watching a group of men work on a building. How odd. My fear began to subside as I saw his smiling face when I drove up. He was actually glad to see me. Sometimes our fear overwhelms our faith, doesn't it? God had obviously prepared this man to receive me, and I was so grateful. I shared with him the contents of the letter and he agreed to take it to the appropriate people. As I drove out of the parking lot, I felt something break off my shoulders and off my back, and I began to weep deeply for over 45 minutes. I couldn't go home because I was so out of sorts that I might have alarmed my wife and children.

Again, I thought that was the end of it but it wasn't! I knew that the most influential man of the group would write something vague to me, failing to take responsibility for his role, and that was exactly what he did. When I received just such a letter, I read it to my wife. She encouraged me to let everything go, and I tried. I wasn't *that* angry about it, or so I thought. I thought I had forgiven all these guys until I came to a conference at Denny Cline's church in Albany, Oregon a few months later and had an odd encounter with a prophet.

During the meeting, the prophet was talking about men and women who had been abused in churches. He called everyone forward who had ever been spiritually abused because God wanted to heal them. I thought, "Hmmm, that's me, I better go." As the prophet approached me, he put his hand on my stomach and told me there was no wound there. I told him that I had been falsely accused and spiritually abused, and he replied that he could find no evidence of it and moved on to the next person. I was so embarrassed. I slunk back to my seat and began to ask God what had just happened.

Later that day, during a break, I was taking a walk and the Lord told me to never view myself as a victim again. He told me that He had healed me of that wound a long time ago, and it was time for me to move on. Wow! I was sick inside over what I was hearing. I repented and began to understand that He had in fact healed me. The problem was that I hadn't totally forgiven the "influential" man who had failed to do what I thought was right. Previously spoken words of rejection and labels had been broken, but my heart still carried a grudge. I had another encounter with the prophet later that day that confirmed God's pleasure in revealing that bit of information to me. It is too complicated to put into words, but it was a very loving encounter that brought me to rest.

When the Holy Spirit had me write the letter, I didn't realize that He desired restoration and reconciliation for everyone involved. Because one man failed to do what I thought he should have, I failed to cancel the debt owed. I was still poisoned, and God used a little bigger stick to bring me into line and freedom. I didn't thank Him at the time, but I do now!

If you take the time to reread the passage that opens this chapter, you will see that being a father isn't about you and me at all. It is about God and His kingdom. We are in a process of dying to ourselves and coming alive to Christ and His kingdom plans. Paul told us in Ephesians 3 that his tribulations were the church's glory. He knew that tribulations were a door to the kingdom, and that they would lead the church close to Christ. He knew that when we willingly die, we are entrusted with more authority. He knew that they were witnessing his pain and that their faith would increase in the process.

The encouraging thing is that all of heaven is waiting to back you up as you choose to be faithful to your purpose and trust Him to help you overcome during seasons of testing. Remember, perfect love casts out fear (1 John 4:18), and nothing can separate us from the love of God (Romans 8:39). The way to overcome is to seek to be a peacemaker and to speak the truth in love. Walk through the process of reconciliation. Let yourself feel the pain of the hurt. Allow the anger to rise up. Then start to seek the Lord and discover how He wants you to respond. You will know you have His heart when your desire for the offender to be right with God and restored is greater than your desire to "make them face what they did!" Then go and do the loving confrontation and see what happens from there. If they own what they did, forgive them. Decide then and there that the debt is cancelled and start to take baby steps in the relationship again. Allow the Lord to heal things and allow trust to be rebuilt.

If the offender fails to own what they did, then forgive them anyway. It is your heart that is at risk here, not theirs.

Sometimes you may need to spend some time listening to them as they tell their side of the story. As you gain information, you may change your mind about the intent and actions of your friend. It is possible that your perspective was wrong, especially if it was based on information or opinion from a third party. Sometimes a big time-out is needed in a relationship because the offender or the offended party just can't get over "it." That's okay. Let God sort this stuff out. He's good at it!

More than once I have been in counseling sessions or in arbitration when I realized that people just weren't ready to deal with each other. It is a very difficult thing to realize that we can't always reflect the love of God to people and see reconciliation come immediately. Sometimes we aren't mature or equipped enough to deal with someone who is badly wounded. Sometimes people are so immature and angry that they have no ability to see their own issues. Some people are so messy that they can't see that they harm those they love. And often, they aren't willing to face it. Sometimes it is best for a Christian to give up and tell God they need some healing and growth to be able to be in relationship with a family member or previously close friend. I have seen numerous people take a time-out from friends and family to go into a season of waiting to improve their boundaries and gain strength, allowing them to pursue reconciliation later.

One final thought: Don't be surprised if the Lord uses an offense to point out unhealed areas of your life that He wants to heal. He seems to major in this. That is why it is so important to seek Him and to be humble enough to see a good Christian counselor when you get hung up on an issue. More often than not, I've found that if I'm still angry after I have tried the other's perspective and worked to reconcile and forgive, there is something deeper to heal. I wish I could tell you that once you are saved all the need for healing just vanishes, but it doesn't. Also, there is no room for denial if you want to be a healthy mom or dad in the kingdom. Getting healed isn't all that bad. After all, it is the Truth who sets you free. Young men in the kingdom learn God's

Word and learn to overcome the evil one. When they learn to deal with persecution and offense, they are overcomers.

Chapter 6

Overcoming Personal Strongholds

"Honor your Father and Mother, as the Lord your God has commanded you, so that you may live long and that it may go well with you in the land the Lord your God is giving you."
Deuteronomy 5:16

"For in the same way you judge others, you will be judged, and with the measure you use, it will be measured to you."
Matthew 7:1

"Do not be deceived; God cannot be mocked. A man reaps what he sows. The one who sows to please his sinful nature will reap destruction; the one who sows to please the Spirit, from the Spirit will reap eternal life."
Galatians 6:7-8

Learning to Apply Truth

In this chapter, I want to describe to you how a stronghold is formed and how to overcome it. Then in the next chapter I'll deal with how to survive and thrive when facing other people's strongholds. Much of what I want to relate to you comes from my experiences in dealing with my own stuff. As you read, please keep in mind these two points: First, it is vital that you deal with strongholds in your life. Second, it is okay to have them. The Lord is gracious and compassionate (Psalm 112:4).

An easy way of defining a stronghold is to simply call it a place in which Satan has influence in your life. A stronghold is composed of a judgment, a bitter expectation, and a vow. At this point I'll introduce an analogy to help you understand the nature of a stronghold. The judgment, which is caused by unforgiveness, is like the outer membrane of a cell. Inside the membrane is the bitter expectation, which is the food that feeds the nucleus of the cell, and the vow is the nucleus. The presence of such cells, or strongholds, influences our heads and hearts. The fruit of strongholds is trouble in our relationships with God and others. I can tell you from experience that the effects vary and seem to be triggered by certain events that arise in our lives.

Ephesians 4:26-27 says:

"Be angry, and do not sin: do not let the sun go down on your wrath, nor give place to the devil."

This verse describes to Christians how to avoid giving the devil a place of influence. When angry, deal with it! And preferably before you go to bed! However, when we are offended and angry, it is common for us to take awhile to deal with the anger. But it is important to choose to forgive as quickly as possible, even if you can't immediately walk through the whole process of forgiveness I described in the last chapter. If we fail to do the forgiving, we will inevitably form a judgment. To get a handle on your personal strongholds, imagine a tree with several branches. On each branch write a word that describes trouble you have had in your life. When I did an inventory like this, I wrote words like rebellion, marital trouble, anger issues, and depression. Next, ask the Holy Spirit what your strongholds are made of and write out a spreadsheet using the three elements I introduced above: judgments, bitter expectations, and vows. After any existing strongholds have been identified, you simply need to ask forgiveness for each of your judgments and bitter expectations. Then ask forgiveness for making a vow in your heart, and finally, renounce that vow. You will be surprised by how much freedom you begin to experience.

I first realized that I had a stronghold in my life during a three-week prayer counseling course I took in June 1997. I will never forget the class session that dealt with strongholds, because it led to an incredible encounter with the love of the Father soon afterward. To God's glory, I have been able to teach this truth to well over a thousand people since, and I have witnessed many healings both here in the United States and in third world nations. This truth is so powerful and I am forever grateful to John and Paula Sanford for their faithfulness to teach so many these life giving tools. So, brace yourself, ask the Father to help you see if you have anything He wants to touch, and then let Him!

The class started like any other. There was the typical milling around and coffee slurping with a sense of anticipation over what we were going to learn. As we began the class, I was a little amazed at how much Scripture was used and at how well the teacher seemed to know it. Though I have a master's degree in counseling, I had never been taught this particular material before. The teacher started out by describing how we, as Christians, develop strongholds in our lives. They often begin during childhood when we are hurt by our mother or father. The Bible tells us that we are to:

"Honor your Father and Mother, as the Lord your God has commanded you, so that you may live long and that it may go well with you in the land the Lord your God is giving you." (Deuteronomy 5:16)

I came to understand that this verse tells us we have the potential to live a long life, and that things will go well for us if we honor our parents. But if we fail to do so, then maybe things wouldn't go so well.

The next verse we looked at was Matthew 7:2

"For in the same way you judge others, you will be judged, and with the measure you use, it will be measured to you."

As our teacher began to expound on this passage, I felt my heart sink. I had already been wrestling with how I had hated my father while growing up, and I knew I hadn't always honored him. Now we were being shown that when we judge, we bring judgment into our own lives. I was really convicted now. I had judged my dad in so many ways. We had been estranged for several years at this point, and I now was wondering what God might be up to. You see, the two Scriptures we looked at so far were like two pieces of twine being twisted together and forming a rope that so many Christians use to hang themselves. There are a couple more strands of twine that help finish our noose, and they are found in Galatians 6:7-8 and Romans 2:1:

"Do not be deceived; God cannot be mocked. A man reaps what he sows. The one who sows to please his sinful nature, from that nature will reap destruction; the one who sows to please the Spirit, from the Spirit will reap eternal life."

"Therefore you are without excuse, every man of you who passes judgment, for in that you judge another, you condemn yourself; for you who judge practice the same things."

As I listened to the teaching, my mind began to go back to my teen years. I had started smoking pot when I was 17, but at that time I generally hated people who drank, because alcohol had adversely affected numerous friends and family. I didn't see the inconsistency of my thinking, but it was occurring to me as I sat in the class that I had chosen to medicate myself with pot but felt free to judge those who drank. I had completed a noose, and I was wearing it!

The teacher then took us through other Scriptures and began to help us learn to overcome our strongholds. Here is how all this works. When we are offended or hurt by people, it is very easy to judge them. Once we judge, we put into play the spiritual law of expansion. Just as the Scripture says that we will be blessed if we do certain things (Matthew 5), it also tells us that we have the capacity to defile many when we become bitter. This is laid out for us in Hebrews 12:14-15 where we are told:

"Pursue peace with all people, and holiness, without which no one will see the Lord: looking carefully lest anyone fall short of the grace of God; lest any root of bitterness springing up cause trouble, and by this many become defiled."

From this we can see that once we judge someone, that judgment can become a bitter root that defiles many. Simply put, I held a lot of judgments against my dad, and they seemed to expand to others who had authority over me. In my employment history, I had several bosses who were less than kind. Though I had always received great evaluations, I had trouble trusting these people, and at the first sign of trouble I wanted out. This is how a single bitter root in our lives can defile many. This situation blooms into a full stronghold once we make a vow in our heart. A vow of the type I am talking about here isn't a good one. It is a statement to God and everyone else, verbalized or not, that you are deciding what will or will not happen in your relationships based on wounding, judgments, and bitter expectations.

An example of this process is the story of the Lord's visit to Abraham in the form of a man with two angels (Genesis 18). When the Lord told Abraham he would have a son, his wife Sarah was listening in on the conversation. She said in her heart that she could not become a mother because she was an old woman. She laughed in her heart, and when she was confronted she denied it. It is easy to see that Sarah and Abraham had long waited on this promise of a son. By the time of the Lord's visit, Sarah had judged God as not keeping His word, and she had become bitter. She then revealed a vow she had made in her heart about what she considered the Lord's poor timing. If we were to diagram the development of Sarah's stronghold, our spreadsheet might look like this:

JUDGMENTS

God didn't keep His earlier promise that we would have children.
God isn't truthful.

BITTER EXPECTATIONS

God didn't come through then, and He probably won't now.

VOWS

I am not going to believe God any further on this matter.

An unhealthy vow, then, is telling God what He can or can't do, or what you are going to allow or not allow in your life, in spite of what His divine will might be. Remember, these types of vows come from painful experiences that go unhealed because we either can't or won't forgive. Now I will share one of my own strongholds and show you how to break your strongholds. I will use the same three categories, "Judgments," "Bitter Expectations," and "Vows," and I will fill in those categories with the appropriate statements.

JUDGMENTS

My dad is unfair.
My dad is uncaring and distant.

BITTER EXPECTATIONS

If my dad is like this, then others in authority will be too.

VOWS

I will not allow anyone in authority to mistreat me.

Before I continue with my account of breaking strongholds, I want to take some time to answer the most common questions that come up when I teach this subject. Folks often ask about the difference between making a judgment and just plain calling a spade a spade. This distinction is difficult because we must use discernment in evaluating who we let close to us and who we don't, as I shared with you in the last chapter. The run-of-the-mill, every day sinner, like most of you reading this, is usually easily forgiven and the relationship is able to go on. When you are dealing with a fool or an evil person, it is an entirely different story. Much of the difference between an honest evaluation and a judgment has to do with how you arrive at your conclusion and what you do with it. If you are angry or bitter at all, then the outcome will likely be a judgment, which indicates you are offended. If you are able to perceive weakness in someone without anger or bitterness, then you've probably made an honest evaluation.

As a counselor and pastor, I often find myself deciding when a person should be trained and released to lead a ministry. When I evaluate them, I want to perceive what the Holy Spirit has to say about them and about what may hinder their success. Are they ready emotionally, spiritually, and mentally to take on ministry? Are they able and willing to take criticism and correction? Are they ready to deal with the trouble that comes with being a leader? If I have judged them in my heart because they have offended me, I usually have less respect, less tolerance and less love for them. If I have that sort of stuff going on inside of me, then I can usually pinpoint a judgment that I have formed against them.

If my evaluation is clean, I find myself concerned for their well-being and I desire them to move into their destiny in God. I am excited for them; this would not be the case if I had a judgment in my heart. Ultimately, when in doubt, confess any thoughts or feelings that seem unclean or tainted by disrespect or bitterness toward that person.

The second most common question that is asked when I teach on this topic has to do with the Scriptures I outlined for you earlier in the chapter. Many people who have been victims of spiritual abuse or abuse by parents or other authority figures often feel that they are justified in their reaction to those who hurt them. They often feel that the Scripture is too harsh or exacting, especially because many hung themselves before they were old enough to understand or be exposed to these truths.

This is a good time to realize that it is okay to be angry. We saw that was the case in Ephesians 4. It is completely normal for us to react to abuse and pain and to become offended. What we often fail to realize is that these verses are intended for our protection and healing. We need to realize that although there was sin against us, if our reaction violates God's Word, we sinned, too. We may not have invited the treatment we received, but if we sin after being hurt, our actions must be dealt with. Our hearts are at stake here. If we are polluted by offense, then we will not live out our potential in Him. We will instead be involved in a reaping and sowing cycle that constantly trips us up. This is not God's will, which is why we were given the revelation we need to overcome these strongholds. Remember, when we ask forgiveness He removes our transgressions from us as far as the east is from the west (Psalm 103:12).

Another important point I'd like to address concerns where strongholds are formed. If you read the book of James, it appears that the battle we face is for our minds. If you read the Psalms, it appears the battle is for our hearts. Either way, minds and hearts are both in the soul realm and, as such, are targets for the enemy. According to 1 Thessalonians 5:23, we are tripartite beings. We have a spirit, a soul, and our body or flesh. There is a constant battle over which part of us will rule. When we have a stronghold in our lives, we often struggle to live by the Spirit. Our flesh and soulish natures rise up and fight our spirit. Even the apostle Paul admitted to this type of struggle in Romans 7.

82

All that said, back to my story. After we left class that day, I really didn't want to do much of anything but go back to my room and do my homework, which was to complete a spreadsheet about judgments, bitter expectations, and vows. As I finished, I knew that I hadn't covered every stronghold in my life, but the teacher told us that God is faithful, as well as merciful, to help us with this process over time. It would be possible to be overwhelmed by the amount of sin and the number of strongholds in our lives if He revealed everything at once. Even though I tried to keep it simple, I filled up a legal-sized page of paper.

After finishing the spreadsheet, I prayed and renounced my vows and asked God to help me avoid forming strongholds in the future. As I lay down on my bunk, I began to sing praises to God by myself for the first time. I didn't know the Scripture back then from Psalm 22:3 which states:

"But You are Holy, Enthroned in the praises of Israel."

When you praise God from your heart, He is enthroned in your midst. He is literally seated on the praise. Wherever He is present, His kingdom can manifest. When we praise from the heart, we invite Him to invade our space. As I worshipped I felt a wonderful peace come over me. I had my eyes closed and was wondering why I had never been able to worship Him alone like this before, when I suddenly felt like the blankets and the mattress folded up all around me. I felt like I was a baby again and God was holding me! I could barely open my eyes to check out the room. When I did, I noticed that the covers were still kicked down at the foot of the bed, and I couldn't move. I literally felt like a baby wrapped to go out in the winter's cold, and I was being held by my Father in heaven. I don't know how long this went on, perhaps about fifteen minutes. As I was being held I felt totally at peace. Soon, the presence of God seemed to lift, and I returned to worshipping Him.

When you have an experience like this, you wonder why. I decided to call my mom and ask her what had happened when I was a baby. She was stunned by my question. I learned that due to circumstances beyond her control soon after my birth, she was sometimes unable to comfort me when I cried. My father, for whatever reason, wanted her to let me cry. He may have been trying to toughen me up (I grew up in Oregon's logging country) or it may have been something else. But it didn't matter anymore. I was amazed by what she shared, and then I started to laugh when I realized that my Heavenly Father knew what I needed and was waiting for the right time to bring my healing. He waited until I had dealt with my anger against my earthly father and then gave me an encounter that revealed His own love for me. After I got off the phone, I couldn't help but marvel at the goodness and mercy of God and His infinite love for us. How can we fail to worship One so gracious and compassionate as He is!

I want to encourage you, whether you are a child, young man, or father in the kingdom, as God nudges you, please do the work needed to gain healing. It is absolutely crucial to be free from strongholds so you are able to help others gain their freedom. Your destiny is to overcome.

Chapter 7

Overcoming Corporate Strongholds

"Then they journeyed from Mount Hor by way of the Red Sea, to go around the land of Edom; and the soul of the people became very discouraged on the way. And the people spoke against God and against Moses: 'Why have you brought us up out of Egypt to die in the wilderness? For there is no food and no water and our soul loathes this worthless bread.' "

Numbers 21:4-5

Learning to Strengthen Yourself and Others

When I meet new people and they find out that I am a pastor, I have noticed I get one of two responses. They usually open up and connect well or they close down. Those who close down often have issues with some leader or authority figure in their past. As we discussed in the last chapter, these judgments take on a life of their own as a single bitter root from a past relationship begins to defile them and others through their unmerited suspicion and fear. Corporate strongholds are often rooted in such individual pain. As a spiritual father, it is very difficult to deal with a discouraged, discontented group of people that has a corporate stronghold. The passage above is just one of many that could have been used to describe what happens when people start to "lose it." As you can see, God and Moses became targets for "discontented followers."

As we learned in the last chapter, as a leader I can get the same treatment from folks that they give their own fathers and mothers. Wounded children too often judge their parents rather than forgive them (Deuteronomy 5:16 and Matthew 7:2). Once they have been offended, they often have "bitter expectations" that every authority will treat them the same way (Hebrews 12:15). A full grown stronghold then blooms when they make a vow in their hearts to "prohibit anyone in authority to ever harm them again." When we run into people with strongholds, whether they are leaders over us or people we are called to father, it can be a messy and fearful thing. Moving forward requires us to have clean hearts and motives, and we need to forgive well. Having thick skin doesn't hurt either!

In the story we have above, the nation of Israel was discontented and discouraged in a big way. This happens a lot in churches and in individual lives. Let's look at how the dynamics of discontentment and discouragement affect groups and individuals. Then I'll discuss how to deal with these circumstances from the position and perspective of a person who is a spiritual father or leader.

The difficulty with corporate strongholds has to do with numbers. An individual who ends up angry and troublesome is easier to deal with than an entire group, because the group draws strength and boldness from within itself, while an individual may be more likely to listen and change course. In Proverbs 13:12 we can see what leads to discontentment and discouragement:

"Hope deferred makes the heart sick, but when the desire comes, it is a tree of life."

People don't just decide one day to be discouraged and discontented. There is a process involved, which can begin when the hopes and dreams of an individual don't come to pass "in a timely manner" (whatever that is). In the passage of Scripture with which we opened this chapter, we saw a group of people that had gone way beyond "heart sickness." In response, God graciously jumped in and bailed Moses out, though we can't expect that particular thing to happen every time. To understand corporate strongholds, it is helpful to describe the process that leads to the kind of trouble we see in the Numbers passage. What happens when people hope for something and it doesn't come about? Well, their hearts get sick. I believe heart sickness begins with some impatience. Impatience seems to breed dissatisfaction, and dissatisfaction seems to press on into creating a critical spirit. When an individual gets a critical spirit, they usually start talking to others. It is easy for others to take on the frustration of the individual. In the course of discussing the problem, the reasons for the problem, and the possible solutions, God and His leader often become the object of their wrath. And since God isn't within eyesight of these folks, guess who gets to listen as they "share"?

In the situation described in the passage above, the people of Israel went from impatience all the way to rebellion. This happened in other places in the Scripture as well. In Numbers 16, Korah and a group of men directly challenged Moses' leadership because of their selfish ambition to promote themselves spiritually and in the sight of the people. Moses was required to both stand up against them and to allow God to intervene on his behalf. When heart sickness degrades all the way to rebellion, you have a bad situation. What so many of us fail to realize is that sin is progressive in nature. It will lead us to destruction if we follow its path. In our original story, the people had become so angry that they must have decided in their hearts (think judgment) that God did not love them, that Moses was a fool, and that the manna was so bad it didn't even qualify as food. Ultimately, they were telling God that their lives were better in Egypt. Now that was a polluted group of people.

As spiritual mothers and fathers, we need a way to help these people as well as ourselves. ***The first step to overcoming discouragement and discontentment is to have an alternate plan, which is contentment.*** Paul gave us some insight into this in Philippians 4:11-13. He told us:

"Not that I speak in regard to need, for I have learned in whatever state I am, to be content; I know how to be abased, and I know how to abound. Everywhere and in all things I have learned to both be full and to suffer need. I can do all things through Christ who strengthens me."

So what is the secret to contentment? ***It is the realization that the power of Christ rests upon you as a covering and within you for strengthening.*** We need to pay attention to Paul's language, too. Contentment is a learned thing and all spiritual fathers need it in their spiritual tool belts. When you are most conscious of personal weakness, He is available. When the enemy attacks you through people, you must learn to retreat back into Christ, not into a defensive position. When things are hard, the enemy wants you to think this is about you and your leadership when in fact the Lord wants you to understand that it is about Christ's sufficiency in you. Contentment isn't self-sufficiency. Contentment is finding yourself in Christ, who is more than enough! Satan wants you to view the issue as being all about you and your shortcomings. God wants you to learn to trust Him. It is really a faith and relationship issue between you and the One who loves you. When you take refuge within yourself where the Holy Spirit resides, and get the peace that He supplies, then and only then can you gain His perspective and clearly display the Father's heart to the people.

The second step in overcoming discouragement and discontentment is ***to realize that contentment brings great freedom.*** Jesus came to set the captives free (Luke 4:18). Therefore, get contentment to gain freedom and you'll have an effective weapon against discouragement and the strongholds that follow. When a person or a group is discontented and covets what they don't have, they fall into the trap of idolatry. Ephesians 5:5 states:

"For this you know, that no fornicator, unclean person, nor covetous man, who is an idolater, has any inheritance in the kingdom of Christ and God."

Idolatry is the death knell to bearing any lasting fruit in the kingdom. This fact should help prevent our wandering so far into discontentment that we reach the point of coveting. Although I have taught our congregation about waiting on the Lord, and how to deal with discouragement and discontentment, I still find trouble in a few. Often they have decided in their hearts that they want something someone else has, and they enter into the bondage of idolatry. Sometimes they just want what they used to have, which is probably a signal that they are in a desert season spiritually and need encouragement.

To learn to wait on the Lord well, meditate on Ecclesiastes 3:1 where we are told:

"For everything there is a season, a time for every purpose under heaven."

In life there is a determined and appointed time for everything. Some who have experience in waiting on the Lord would tell you that waiting is merely a precise, short-term season during which God's purposes come about. It rarely feels short-term to most of us, though. Sometimes He is extremely merciful to define this period for us, and other times we simply must wait.

I'll illustrate this point with a personal experience. I had a vision back in October 1997 that I won't ever forget. For about four months after I had returned from the Elijah House Prayer Counseling School, I heard from the Lord in incredible ways. One morning while sitting at my desk waiting for my first client to arrive, I was in prayer and began to see a strange event. I saw

Jesus standing in a desert storm, yelling something to me that I couldn't hear over the sound of the wind. As I strained to hear Him, the Holy Spirit reminded me that Jesus could calm storms (Mark 4:39). I cried out for Him to calm the storm so I could hear His voice. He did so. He then proceeded to tell me that though I wouldn't hear from Him like I had been, He would never leave me or forsake me. He seemed to be smiling as He said these words. Then the vision faded.

I sat there awhile wondering what He meant. We had been having so much fun, or so I thought, and now he was calling time-out. I wondered whether the time-out would last a few hours or a few days or what? Little did I know I was facing nine months of desert time. I grew confused as days went by and I didn't hear His still, small voice. I thought perhaps I had done something wrong to displease Him. It was a lonely and confusing time that ultimately led to frustration and even anger. I had never heard of people going through a "desert" time before and had no idea I was in one. I didn't understand that waiting on the Lord had so many benefits. When you are forced to wait you actually have an opportunity to better understand and know God and yourself. As you feed on the Word and as the Holy Spirit guides you, you will find yourself tripping over things in your heart that aren't clean, and ultimately you will perceive the constant need to repent. If you aren't open to correction during these desert seasons, you will take many trips around the mountain until you are.

Often the things the Lord will speak to you will test you (Psalm 105:19). Once you stop fighting and become silent, you can learn and accept what is true about yourself and about Him. That is why we are told in Psalm 46:10:

"Be still and know that I am God; I will be exalted among the nations, I will be exalted in the earth!"

When you are in a desert season, remember above all else to keep pursuing Him. One very helpful Scripture to keep in mind during the desert times is found in Psalm 37:4-5:

"Delight yourself also in the Lord and He shall give you the desires of your heart. Commit your way to the Lord, trust also in Him, and He shall bring it to pass."

It is incredibly important to discipline yourself and your mind while you wait. Try hard to avoid becoming God's accuser during the seasons of waiting in your life. It is good to focus on prayer and to learn to love God and others better during these hard seasons. At least then you are fulfilling some of the commandments. Besides, learning to love is usually what He is trying to teach you anyway.

My desert season ended when I attended a conference featuring John Paul Jackson, John Sanford, and Mark Dupont in August 1998 in Spokane. I was stunned and fascinated to hear my first teaching on living in a "spiritual desert." I also received a prophetic word from a team of men and women that John Paul was mentoring. It was an incredible way to break a drought. God was in the details of that word, and I left the conference with a much deeper understanding of Him and His love.

In summary, learn contentment and you will have freedom. To learn contentment, learn first that God's timing is perfect. Be still before Him and delight yourself in Him. And learn to wait, contentedly.

*Let's look at the third step to overcoming discontentment and discouragement: **catch it early**.* When we fail to catch it early, we do what Israel did in our Numbers 21 passage. They had been given freedom from Egypt but they slid into discouragement, and sour words soon followed. They complained that freedom wasn't satisfactory after all; they pined for their old life of slavery along the Nile. We can be just like them, calling evil good and good evil.

91

I remember a time when God chose to honor a friend of mine and I felt that it was unjust. I heard what was coming from my heart and immediately began to repent. In Luke 6:45 we are told that:

". . . out of the abundance of the heart his mouth speaks."

If I hadn't caught it early, I would have failed to rejoice with my friend (Romans 12:15) and probably would have complained to others about the situation. In the process, I would have lost favor in the group and probably lost the trust of my friend. Eventually, I realized that I had waited a long time for recognition but it was my friend's time, not mine. It was good to experience hearing my heart even though it was painful. In this case I had begun the process of becoming offended long before I was aware of it. As Jeremiah said in chapter 17, verse 9, our hearts are very difficult to understand sometimes, aren't they?

A fourth step to overcoming discontentment and discouragement is *choose to be patient*. Did you realize that patience is a choice? Satan desires to confuse us on this point. He wants us to allow circumstances to define reality as though the current situation is permanent. You know the expression "it isn't over until the fat lady sings." Well, don't fixate on hearing the "spiritual fat lady" launch into an aria. (You probably won't recognize the song anyway. Or she'll call in sick.) Instead, remember patience and allow God to rule; let Him write your present and your future. The truth is that those who hope in God will not be disappointed. When we allow ourselves to become discontented, or discouraged, we tend to come to premature conclusions about where we are going and what our potential in Christ is. And premature conclusions make you drop the book before the story ends. If satan can make you believe it is all over, you have abandoned your hope in God.

The fifth key to overcoming discontentment and discouragement is to **believe His promise to be your helper.** Don't help yourself to what you want. He is present with you even when things feel bad. Don't let circumstances define reality. It is too easy to begin to fear the future and to forget that He supplies your daily needs. What He has spoken He will do! Resist hardening your heart. Tests are tests. Israel was tested in the desert, and many of us have been tested there as well. The desert times are there to build your faith and to make you hungry and thirsty for His presence. Remember what happens to those who hunger and thirst for righteousness? They get filled! It is during these desert experiences that we are healed and delivered from selfish ambition and lies that have dominated our view of ourselves, God, and the world.

When a desert season passes, you will find new vision and purpose. So for now, sit at His feet and find the peace and truth He so desires to give you. So many of us are striving to see our destinies come to pass, and in doing so we miss a key spiritual principle of entering His rest. We must learn and remember what God has said and what He has done for us. David had to do this.

In 1 Samuel 30, we find David in deep trouble with his own men because their city, Ziklag, had been burned and looted. Their wives, children and animals had been taken by the Amalekites, and it says in verses 4 and 6 that:

"David and the men who were with him lifted up their voices and wept until they had no more power to weep . . . Now David was greatly distressed, for the people spoke of stoning him because the soul of all the people was grieved."

In this situation, grief overtook the men, and David did something very significant. He didn't panic; he didn't run; he didn't tell the men that he had been the only one who was willing to take them in when they were debtors and discontented. He didn't demand loyalty and begin to fight with those who were against him. Instead it simply says "but David strengthened himself in the Lord." He then sought help from the priest, sought

God on behalf of himself and his people, and then pursued the issue, recovering all.

The key to ultimately overcoming the strongholds and trouble from others is found in this passage. You, like David, must know how to "strengthen yourself in the Lord." We don't know exactly what David did to strengthen himself, but the Scripture gives us some hints.

David had spent an enormous amount of time alone with God as a young man when he watched over his father's flocks. During that time he had killed at least one lion and a bear. He had come to know God in an intimate way so he was faith filled and fearless. David had also overcome his brothers' false accusations of arrogance when he volunteered to take on the giant called Goliath.

When David killed Goliath, he gained favor with Saul. That favor soon turned to murderous hatred for David when Saul perceived that the people saw David as greater than he. David spent the better part of the next 10 to 12 years being chased around the desert by a mad man. Along the way, he managed to resist the temptation to take Saul's life and create his own way to the throne when Saul unwittingly entered a cave in which David was hiding. As a youth and as a leader of men, David had seen God protect him and cause him to prosper in numerous situations. David had a call and anointing to be king, and he must have remembered this when he "strengthened himself in the Lord."

How many times have you poured your heart into people only to have them turn on you? How have you handled it in the past? Speaking for myself, I had a long process of coming around to do what David did. In my history I have entertained the thought of quitting several times. I've thought of running and waiting for things to blow over. I've even thought of ways to placate people so there could be "peace" when things were hard. But ultimately God desires us to trust Him, stand up, and to lead. He longs to manifest His help and strength to us in our times of trouble. Psalm 33:20-22 says:

"Our soul waits for the Lord; He is our help and our shield. For our heart shall rejoice in Him, because we have trusted in His holy name. Let Your mercy , O Lord, be upon us, just as we hope in You."

These are things David must have remembered when he "strengthened himself in the Lord." A father in the kingdom must have a deep relationship with God to draw on as well as a good memory when this level of warfare occurs. It is necessary to remember God's promises to you whenever you are shaken. It is necessary to strengthen yourself in God. He approves of you. He loves you. He wants to show Himself strong on your behalf.

I had the privilege of watching some of my spiritual fathers overcome large obstacles in ministry when I was a young man in the kingdom. Their lessons became my lessons. It is so important for a young man in the kingdom to see how to overcome. Learning to overcome is a requirement if they are to become spiritual fathers worth emulating.

Sometimes God shows Himself to us and helps to strengthen us when we are simply seeking to position ourselves to receive His help. God knows when extra grace is required. And extra grace is exactly what God gave to me during a dark season in my life. At that time my family took a trip to Disneyland. It didn't seem like the best idea to me at the time, but we had promised the kids for years that we would take them, and someone had just given us $2000 for the trip. I was very depressed and thought we should plan to stop in Redding, California on our way down and on our way back so I could attend church at Bethel where Bill Johnson is pastor. I had heard tons of wonderful things about Bill and his church and hoped I might be able to get some prayer for my issues during ministry time.

When we arrived I could feel God's presence even out in the parking lot. Needless to say, this was just the warm welcome that I needed. They didn't even need greeters, though they had them, because I knew God was there. As we entered the building, I ran into a prophet named Larry Randolf who had ministered in our church about six months prior, and he introduced me to Bill with whom we had a brief, fun chat. Before I took my seat, I asked Larry if they would be having ministry time at the end of the service. He assured me they would, and as I left him I felt hopeful to receive a touch from God.

The sermon was simple and powerful. The atmosphere was warm and loving, and the Lord moved among the people as Bill taught us the importance of hearing God's voice. When the sermon ended, the ministry teams were called forward and I was relieved to see so many of them. The place was packed and I found myself moving in a crowd to try to find someone to pray for me. I happened to be on the far right side of the room and as I moved forward I kept drifting further to my left searching for an available prayer team member. I eventually worked my way over to the very last prayer team member. He was a large man, about my age and very kind. I must have passed by at least 60 occupied prayer team members to finally arrive in front of this man.

As I stood there, he asked me how I was doing. I wasn't sure how to answer because I didn't want him to know I was a pastor; I was afraid he might have issues with that. It has been my experience that lay people don't treat pastors the same as others. They get nervous, or fail to perceive pastors as human with needs, just like them. I stuttered and stumbled over my words as I spoke. I finally blurted out that I was depressed and was facing major decisions that would affect my family's future. Inside I was hoping that would be enough information to move him to pray. As I bowed my head, I heard the Lord say, "Tell him more." I looked back up at this kind man and said, "Okay, look. I am a pastor in a church that has people in it that don't like me, don't want me to be their pastor, and I am considering quitting. I am exhausted, depressed, and angry with the group, and I need to hear from God about what to do." I dropped my head again, took a deep breath, and looked back up at him only to be amazed that a tear was falling down his cheek. He looked at me and said, "About three years ago I was pastoring a church that chewed me up and spit me out. I came here to heal from my own wounds and recently started a ministry that focuses on healing pastors."

You could have pushed me over with a feather. I began to weep as he reached out and gave me a big bear hug. Only months before, Bob Jones had prophesied to me that God had been pleased to birth our little church. He told me that she was a beautiful baby girl, but when the tulips bloom in the spring, He would birth a baby boy with authority. I hadn't understood the word when Bob gave it, but I was about to understand it now.

After this kind and gentle man prayed over me for a little while, I felt many hands on my back and head. I heard Larry's voice tell me that he had found a bunch of intercessors to pray for me. As they prayed, I felt the peace and power of God come on me. I fell to the floor under the weight of it and found that I couldn't even open my eyes. As they prayed and prophesied, I was beginning to sense that I needed something beyond that which I was already receiving. When their prayers had ceased one woman added, "Steve, there is one more thing that God wants you to know: the flowers have bloomed." All I could do was weep. I knew that the word from God's prophet was coming to pass and that I would be alright. I had been depressed, confused, and frustrated when I arrived at Bethel that morning. When I finally was able to get off the floor, I understood that learning to overcome trials of discouragement and discontentment seasons us for fatherhood in the kingdom. During such trials, resist allowing the enemy to exploit your issues; satan will escalate them into a corporate stronghold, if he can. Get contentment, get freedom. Catch the problem early, choose to be patient and to receive God's help.

In the next chapter I want to look at what our "big picture" purpose is when we father in the kingdom. When we understand the goal for our lives and for the lives of those we mentor, we can confidently accept our mission: know Him, become like Him, and give Him away!

Part Three

What Fathers Do:
How to Father, What to Teach and Model

Chapter 8

Understanding Your Calling and Mission

"When You said, 'Seek My face,' My heart said to You, 'Your face, Lord, I will seek.' "

Psalm 27:8

"For whom He foreknew, He also predestined to be conformed to the image of His Son, that He might be the firstborn among many brethren."

Romans 8:29

"Go therefore and make disciples of all the nations, baptizing them in the name of the Father and of the Son and of the Holy Spirit."

Matthew 28:19

Getting and Keeping a Clear Purpose

Before we planted Desert Rock Fellowship in April 2000, Pam and I had the pleasure of going to a "church planters' boot camp." It was put on by the Foursquare Church denomination in a beautiful setting near Troutdale, Oregon. When Pam and I went we had little or no idea that we would be planting a church, but God knew! It was November 1999 and we were in a season of wondering what God might be up to. Jon Brandstetter, one of my favorite pastors and friends, had invited me to come to the boot camp as he had seen me wrestle with where I was in my life and wanted to be helpful. He could see that God might be moving me,

101

even if I didn't. The leadership at Bethel Church where I served, graciously allowed me extra time off to explore this opportunity. When we got to the camp we were treated like one of their own. We were given a large welcome basket with T-shirts and fruit, as well as other gifts, and we were greeted with open arms in every way.

During the course of the week, we literally "planted a church on paper." We were instructed on how to come up with purpose statements, church values, strategies, marketing, and everything else that might be needed along the way. It was a wonderfully enlightening and challenging week. As the week closed we were laughing at how our "new church" would look, while wondering why we "did all that work for nothing." The man in charge of the boot camp told Pam and I to stay where we were until God moved us. We were told that we had all the qualifications necessary to plant, but it needed to be in God's timing. We were more than happy to receive that word because planting a church was not on our agenda.

After boot camp, I jumped back into my ministry as a counselor, and Pam continued to work as a homemaker, Sunday school teacher, and mom. It wasn't but a couple of months later that we began to see why God had sent us to boot camp. I had a faint, but growing awareness through a number of issues that God might be preparing me to leave Bethel, but I wasn't quite getting the message. A few months before attending the boot camp we had visited a Vineyard church while in Oregon, and the pastor's wife had told us that God was calling us out and that we needed to take a step forward as a sign of faith and obedience. When I stepped forward, I immediately went out in the Spirit and landed on my back where I stayed for about 15 or 20 minutes. For those of you who haven't had this experience, I wasn't hurt. God was just trying to get my attention. I am embarrassed to say that I still was a little slow on the uptake. Remember, I am not the sharpest tack in the box!

Part of my problem was that I was a reluctant father. At some level I would have been content to stay at Bethel until retirement. The church is filled with wonderful people and the elders made sure our financial, retirement, and health care needs were beautifully met. It was fun being the counselor in a church of over 2000 people. I had been given the freedom to create and implement a lay counselor program. I had the opportunity to serve with some incredible men of God. Bethel was a grace in so many ways. The thought of leaving was scary.

Everything came into focus when I delivered a sermon on the first Sunday in January 2000. I had received our senior pastor's okay to do the sermon, but I knew in my heart it might be my last. I spoke out of Psalm 63 on seeking God's face in the sanctuary. God showed up that day. One man had to be prayed over for a number of minutes before he could move. He was literally frozen to his seat. After the first service, a number of people were crying, and my senior pastor told me that what I had done was very brave. He was obviously touched by it. We had numerous people stop us at Costco and Home Depot that afternoon to tell us how wonderful the sermon was. Our phone rang off the hook because people were excited about the possibility of a move of God.

By the time I preached the Psalm 63 sermon, I suspected a transition was already in the works. I sensed that God had given me a new vision and a new direction. Moving into the role of a spiritual father would be evidenced by my leaving Bethel to plant a new church. While at Bethel I had ideas I wanted to implement that in reality were not for me to decide or initiate. I lost favor through my persistence and frustration (which I should have), because where there is more than one vision, there is division. I wasn't mature enough to see that, but the elders were. So we left Bethel, and I am very grateful then and now for how they have blessed us with their old building and for the relationships we still have. I am honored to serve God with them in our city. Because they have been true to their God-given vision, we at Desert Rock are free to express our vision. We both fill needed and necessary roles here in southeastern Washington.

When we planted Desert Rock we implemented our "boot camp" church planting plan. But somewhere along the way I began to doubt what we were doing. These doubts grew into dissatisfaction and discontentment. I don't think I ever let it progress to full-blown "heart sickness" like we discussed in the last chapter, but I sure wasn't a happy camper. As a spiritual father it is too easy to focus on numbers, on major victories and on what God is doing in the realm of the miraculous in your midst. But when you think things are too quiet, the situation can become very painful, especially when you lose focus on what is important. Needless to say, I had a lot of questions about life, ministry, and relationships. I wanted some answers, and thankfully I wasn't alone. I have friends who pastor in four different states and some of them have also had "the grumblies."

I had a memorable conversation with one of those pastors. He lamented the maturity level of the people in his congregation and he was concerned that they had become apathetic and shallow. He was struggling to figure out how to encourage them to move forward. In this effort, he found that many of the older members felt like they had done enough and wanted to go into cruise control. They expected the young people in the congregation to pick up the load because, after all, it was their turn. Whoa! This particular church had plenty of people, but few spiritual fathers and mothers. My opinion may not have been right, but I was familiar enough with the church to believe that their focus had become too one-dimensional, just like mine.

It's so easy to get off track, isn't it? *In Christendom today, it is very common for us to become task driven and relationship poor.* It is easy to focus on things in the natural and to forget the spiritual. Churches are famous for organizing new programs and encouraging folks to participate. What this spiritual father and I were up against as pastors was all too common. Believers still feel

104

a need to perform to please our Father and men. When we do this long enough, we wear out and give up. Spiritual children walk along forgetting, or maybe never learning, that the Father in heaven loves them unconditionally. Without a sense of acceptance based on love, we perform and work until we give up or become old and religious. Our lack of intimacy with the Father stunts growth and keeps us from the freedom that comes when we experience the love of the Father. My "grumblies" were no different than my brothers'. I had failed to see that God was dealing with people in our church and with me. We had been going backward in numbers, and I didn't see it as a pruning, but instead as rejection.

I had tried to do my best, but my best didn't bear the kind of fruit I was looking for. I was lonely and depressed and needed some answers. All the Bible school, seminary, and church planter's boot camps couldn't help me. I needed a fresh revelation from God. Fortunately He knew that better than I did, and He showed His grace to me once again.

The encounter came very unexpectedly. I was in my office writing "yet another sermon" when I became aware in my spirit that the presence of God was about to enter my office. I always hope that He is present with me when I write sermons, but this was much more intense. My body started shaking so I decided to drop my pen so I wouldn't hurt myself. I didn't know what was going to happen, but I figured at least I was gaining a first hand understanding of why the Quakers were called the Quakers!

At the most intense moment of the encounter, I heard the voice of the Lord speak into my spirit. His voice was very clear, and the message was very precise. He said,

"Success in the kingdom begins with getting to know Me [Jesus], becoming like Me, and then taking as many people with you as you can."

When He had finished speaking, I worked up the nerve to ask Him several questions. Some were about why we hadn't seen the things we had hoped for. He comforted and reassured me that we would see the things we had been praying about in time, and that everything was going to be okay. After He had graciously answered all of my questions, the Spirit lifted.

It was a wonderful and peaceful encounter in spite of all the shaking. When I finally settled down, I just burst out laughing at the profound, yet simple truth the Lord had given me. In fact, as I sat there I became aware that I had received a perfect "purpose statement" for any Christian to live by. Our church now has this purpose statement hanging on two banners in our sanctuary, and we are planning to post them in the foyer, as well.

If you will peek back at the three Scriptures I gave you at the beginning of this chapter, you will notice how they correspond with the words Jesus gave me in my encounter. To become a father you must be intimate. It is too easy to focus on the task of "making disciples" and on the effort to train people to "be conformed" to Christ without first seeking His face. *When you father people in the kingdom, the most important thing to teach them is to seek the presence of God. When you major on "task" and skimp on "relationship," the product will be shallow and ultimately fruitless.* Intimacy brings insight, anointing, and freedom. Being task-oriented brings weariness, shallowness, and bondage. I had forgotten the big picture. I am here to "know" Him and to worship Him. So are you. The rest of the stuff should flow from that. I had forgotten this truth during the first few years of birthing Desert Rock, and I needed to get my house in order again.

When we seek God, we find Him. When we find Him, we can be conformed to His image. We are conformed to His image through knowledge and experience gained through intimacy. We then begin to understand the heart of the Father and adopt His perspectives as our own. When you father and mentor, please always model a hunger for God's presence. Keep a dynamic and consistent time set aside for Him. If you don't, your task of fathering will become dry because you will be giving and giving and people will be taking and taking, and you will find yourself lacking.

When I am as disciplined as I should be, I take a 30- to 60-minute walk four or five times a week. I try to pray in the Spirit the majority of that time. I then try to spend time in our prayer room at church four or five times a week to just soak. Soaking in God's presence is simple. Find some worship music you really enjoy and get comfortable . . . meditate on Him, the words of the songs, or sing an entirely new song to Him. Do whatever it takes to just spend time listening.

In May of 2005 we set up a 24/7 prayer room. We began the prayer room with the goal of praying for seven days straight before a conference we were hosting. In the process, the church wanted to keep it going. So we did! The prayer room still exists today. I highly recommend that you have a place like this in your home or in your church.

At our prayer room, you sign up for a certain time slot on any day that works for you. We are careful to avoid disturbing each other while in the room. The sign up board is outside the room, making it is easy to check if someone is in there or not. Because spending large amounts of time with God isn't always easy, we have tried to simplify it. When you enter the room, we have you sign into a book and briefly write down what God has placed on your heart for you to pray over. You may also record any insights God gives you, to be read by those who follow you. We have musical instruments, an artist's easel, and butcher paper on the walls. You may come in and do artwork as a form of prayer and worship to God. You are invited to write your prayer requests on the walls, as well as on rocks that we have provided so that you can take them as a reminder to pray for an issue or to leave behind for others to pray about. We have a small refrigerator for storing our communion elements so that you can come in and have communion. During dry times it helps to have plenty of options as you wait on the Lord.

Spending time is the only way I know to get close to someone, including God. To become a father in the kingdom, you must get close to God — it is a requirement. Find what works for you and go for it! Those you mentor and father will receive the greatest gift you can give . . . relationship with the Father.

Chapter 9

Fathering, Mentoring, and Leading

*"Do not rebuke an older man, but exhort him as a father,
younger men as brothers, older women as mothers,
younger women as sisters, with all purity."*
1 Timothy 5:1

Tools for Nurturing Others

Fathers in the kingdom have grown to "know" God
intimately and have learned to overcome the evil one. As fathers,
they then help birth others into their destinies. Whether they are
nurturing an individual, a home group, a children's ministry, a
men's group, or an entire church, they see their kingdom role as an
outflow of intimacy with God. The true spiritual father finds time
to lovingly teach, counsel, discipline, and encourage spiritual sons
and daughters. Whenever a mentoring relationship begins, the
relationship should be defined by the Holy Spirit, but the
particulars of what it looks like should be negotiated between the
parties involved.

When you sense that God is calling you to pour into a son
or a daughter, you must realize that you may have a limited
amount of time and influence in their lives. Be aware of what God
wants you to instill and be equally aware of the son's or daughter's
expectations; both of these aspects are very important pieces of a
relational puzzle. Obviously, fathering or mentoring requires
relationship, and a healthy relationship requires appropriately

defined boundaries. When you enter into a fathering relationship with those God highlights for you, you are raising up sons and daughters, not interns and students. Being a spiritual father to a spiritual son is intentionally far more personal than having a congregation member attend your Sunday school class or sit in a pew as you preach. Mentoring is far more relational than leading, teaching, or pastoring. Let me attempt to explain why.

In my mind, there is a big difference between fathering or mentoring and leading. If you are a Sunday school teacher, small group leader, or a pastor you usually have the spiritual authority to implement your vision. The relationship you have with the group you oversee is limited, because people come to church for many reasons and some go home with little or no desire to be known by or accountable to anyone. The same is true of small groups; however, some folks attend church or small groups because they have a genuine desire for relationship and growth in their faith. You cross the line from leading to fathering when you intentionally commit to a spiritual father/son relationship. You cannot father or mentor people who don't want it. Undertaking a mentoring relationship requires intimacy, commitment to growth, permission for you to speak into the person's life, and on their part, an openness to be corrected.

Now, leaders play an important role in the body of Christ. Without them we are doomed for chaos and rebellion. *Every leader should be a father, but he won't be a father to all those he leads.* When you lead a small group, you may have one or two people who ask for more time with you. As you get to know one another, it may become apparent that these relationships have a deeper, mentor/son potential. Ask the Holy Spirit what He is doing in the person's life who is seeking help to grow. And ask the spiritual son or daughter what they are looking for. If you fail to do either of these, there could be trouble later.

The relationship you form may have established goals or you may just choose to hang out. Either way, allow the Holy Spirit to guide you both into a relationship that He speaks through. The cross over from leading to fathering occurs when you move from teaching and overseeing to an intentionally deeper, more personal commitment. This includes being available to listen when there are painful issues going on in a son or daughter's life and to give counsel when needed. No matter what the relationship looks like, you need to be ready to go through growing pains in yourself and in those you father.

As a father, note that our opening Scripture for this chapter gives crucial counsel concerning how to relate to various people groups within the church. Treating people with humility and respect is a must. I have seen too many sick relationships in the church to fail to address this here. Jesus is God. You are not! I find it mind blowing to see "fathers" have their spiritual sons and daughters carry their suitcases, wash their cars, or come to their homes and wash their windows, all under the guise of teaching them to be servants. Jesus modeled servanthood, so should you! Maybe the father should wash the son's car? We have too many spiritual prima donnas running around. The Bible says in Matthew 10:8:

"Heal the sick, cleanse the lepers, raise the dead, cast out demons. Freely you have received, freely give!"

A true spiritual father will recognize that he is but dust, and he will be compelled to give away what the Lord has given him. We are all needy, and that need doesn't stop at salvation. A person who exalts himself will be brought down. A person who is humble will be raised up. Fathering and mothering in the kingdom is about nurturing and raising up healthy servants of the Most High. They will likely become what they see. Let them see Jesus in you as much as possible.

When you mentor someone, please treat them with respect and honor. You are not entering a normal parent/child relationship like you did when you had babies in the natural. Be prepared to deal with them in adult-to-adult terms. Most errors in mentoring occur in the relationship, not in doctrine. Bad experiences led one well known Christian to remark on a syndicated program that the Holy Spirit is all you need. Evidently she had seen enough. I totally understand the reasons for her statement, but I grieve that it was said. The Holy Spirit *is* a great teacher, but the Holy Spirit has chosen to use *us* as a vehicle to help others learn about God and to experience Him.

A couple of years ago, I was mentoring two distinct groups of men in my church. One group consisted of younger men and the other of older men. In the younger men's group we laid a foundation on how to know the difference between relationship with God and religion, and on how authority works in the kingdom. I assigned them books such as *There Were Two Trees in the Garden* by Rick Joyner and *A Tale of Three Kings* by Gene Edwards. We also worked on how to hear God's voice, and I had them practice listening to God by prophesying to each other. In forming this group, I invited six or seven guys with the idea that I would be able to develop friendships with them and among them, while helping each of them learn some basics in the faith. Out of that group, I hoped to have one or two who went further with me in a more intimate father/son type of relationship. All of them have very significant calls of God on their lives, and I want more than anything to see Christ formed in them (Galatians 4:19). Today one of them is pastoring a home group with me, and another is preparing to move on to be involved in youth ministry. I believe at least two of the young men from the group will eventually be involved in missionary work.

In the older men's group, we did things differently. About a dozen men were invited, and about seven stuck it out. In that group we had a more mature set of participants, and I had felt led to help draw out of them spiritual lessons that they had learned. Our stated goals for this group were to help one another through mutual encouragement, to inspire each other to father in the kingdom, and to cover each other through prayer.

When we met the first time, I had each man answer a set of questions about fathering at home and in the kingdom that sent us on a journey of discovering the heart of God for spiritual fatherhood. I asked them what successes they had in the past as fathers at home and in the kingdom. I also asked them why they thought they had been successful. I then asked them what failures they had experienced as fathers at home and in the kingdom. I asked them what they thought caused the failures and what they learned in the process. Homer, the Greek poet, understood the value of failure and crisis when he said, "Adversity has the effect of eliciting talents which in prosperous circumstances would have lain dormant."

In the last part of this chapter I want to share ten lessons learned by the men in the older group, lessons they hadn't even been aware of before our sessions. As the men shared, one of them wrote what each guy had to say on butcher paper on my office wall. We found there was a tremendous amount of wisdom in the room. We all have many spiritual lessons tucked away that we need to learn to pull out and use. If we can learn to do this, then we will be more effective as spiritual fathers in the kingdom. See if you can relate to what the men at Desert Rock have learned about fathering in the home and in the kingdom.

Our first two lessons were *fathering is a commitment to relationship for better or worse* and try to *teach those who are teachable*. Most of the guys had come to realize that you are either a father or you aren't. Fathering your natural children or spiritual children takes a gritty commitment that is unshakable if you are going to accurately reflect the Father's heart to His people. Even the prodigal son, though let go, was more than allowed back when he repented. The father celebrated! You can't pick your own kids, but you do have some say in which ones you choose to mentor. Be sure their commitment to be mentored is as strong as yours is to pour into them. It isn't enough to see that someone has a messy life and to realize you're the one to help. The potential son or daughter must see their own need; both parties must be ready and committed if the relationship is going to work.

Our third lesson was **character counts.** The character qualities needed to father are many and diverse. Consider these: love, patience, unselfishness, courage, ability to nurture, strength, and integrity.

Love carries the qualities of hope, endurance, and faith in the people you are helping and rooting for. One time I had a leader completely fail to be responsible to take care of very important issues that I had entrusted him with. What caused his fall was a relapse into an addiction he had supposedly overcome. I will never forget looking at him in my office and thinking that "Murder isn't an option, but what else is there?" I was able to remain silent until I could lovingly help him come up with a plan to get further healing and then figure out how to clean up the mess he had made. Thankfully I remembered how patient God had been with me over the years, and I knew that what this man needed was love, not my temper.

Whether you are dealing with a terrible-two-year-old or a teenager, you must have a bunch of *patience.* This is also true when you are mentoring someone who struggles with addictions to alcohol or pornography. Without patience we will fail to reflect the heart of God. In Psalm 103:8 the Scripture tells us:

"The Lord is merciful and gracious, slow to anger and abounding in mercy."

I have some old farmer wisdom listed on a sheet of paper above my computer monitor. One of my favorite lines is, "Don't wrestle with pigs: you'll get all muddy and the pigs will love it." Another favorite is, "Words that soak into your ears are whispered, not yelled." Being *patient* helps you to avoid reacting in frustration and allows you to act upon things in a godly manner.

Another key character quality listed by most of the older men was ***unselfishness***. It is nearly impossible not to come face to face with your own selfishness about the time your firstborn comes home with you. Maybe you need to help your wife with chores or "baby-sit" (which goes over like Mother's Day in an orphanage), if that's what you choose to call taking care of your own child. If your thoughts and concerns are all about you and what you desire, then you will find parenting at home or in the kingdom too tedious, and you'll end up stinking at it. To overcome selfishness, lay down your life, and learn to die to yourselves (it will be painful, and you may not like it, but it is what is necessary). Carve out time to spend with God, and so fill your tank with spiritual gas that "self" will be flushed out. I like to repeat a mantra when I feel like I am not getting my due, "It's not about you, it's about the kingdom." When you are content and filled with God's Spirit, you will be most likely to focus on His agenda, not your own.

Courage was another character quality we thought was required to father well. Don't be afraid of confrontation (often required) or transparency (also required) or of making mistakes (you probably will). All the guys had learned in some measure to trust God with scary situations and to step out in faith knowing that He is faithful. One of the most interesting stories in the Scriptures is about David killing the giant. While watching his father's flocks, he had learned to trust God when he had to kill the lion and the bear. Not many of us will have to kill lions or bears, but confronting others and risking rejection can sure feel daunting. Learning to love God and others more than yourself helps overcome these types of fears.

Our next character quality was the ability to ***nurture without controlling.*** The men decided that a healthy father had to have a desire to let young men succeed and stand on their own. This insight was gained partly because some had experienced spiritual abuse in the past. The "shepherding movement" of the 70s, which was an extreme form of control, in some cases led to pastors telling people who they should marry and exercising public chastisement for failure to tithe. These instances are severe, yet they occurred. Most controlling behavior in churches and families doesn't go quite that far. As a father, whether natural or spiritual, know that the quickest way to shut down a relationship is to manipulate or demand that your son or daughter do things your way through emotional blackmail or threat. Remember to look at what God is doing with them in the big picture, and let them become who they are, which will not be a junior you.

Another asset we discovered we needed as spiritual fathers was **personal strength**. As we discussed our past fathering opportunities, we realized we had to have a secure view of our relationship with God and be confident as spiritual mentors or we were ineffective. Some of the men reported having been in situations where their successes were viewed as a threat by those in authority over them. In response, the men who were in those circumstances hid some of their achievements and some moved on to safer environments. In such cases, the focus of the spiritual fathers was on promoting their ministries and looking good, not on raising up young men and women.

Finally, the heaviest word on our list of needed character qualities was **integrity**. In my world, integrity has a higher value than anointing. During the last 20 or 30 years, we've all wished that the men and women of influence in the kingdom had more of this. Every time we turn around, the media is highlighting yet another man who has broken the rules and fallen into sin. And on a more personal level, haven't we all ached over the poor examples we've been to our kids at home? There probably isn't anyone reading this who doesn't regret choices made and consequences endured at some point in their lives. I am very grateful to have a bunch of people around me who have integrity and commitment to keep it.

For believers in general and for fathers specifically, it is impossible to overstate that strong character is essential. I won't allow people to step into leadership roles in our church until I am convinced they have strong, godly character and will treat people with respect. When you are a father, your mission is to rally young men and women in the faith to move into intimacy with God. Having developed godly character yourself, you will inspire confidence among your children that intimacy with God is real and achievable.

Following character, the fourth lesson coming from the "mature set" on being a successful father was *give away your time and your love liberally.* As an example, I was in a situation when I was 19 where I needed lots of time, grace, and patience. My first spiritual dad, Charlie Fischer, was exactly what I needed. He was always available to me. I went over to his house constantly, but never felt like I was a burden or in the way. He and his wife, Kaye, were so loving and welcoming that I began to look at God differently because of my experiences with them.

Looking back, I'm thankful for the gift of their time. So let me ask, "Do you have time to father? Are you available?" These days we need to seek a balance in our schedules. We can so easily say "yes" to commitments that we find ourselves scheduled down to the second, feeling pressured and overburdened. Then we become stingy with our minutes, unable and unwilling to give when our time with someone could be critical for them. Sadly, I have watched young men and women in the faith ask for time only to be told there wasn't any. Ouch! Just yesterday I got a call from a young man in my congregation who wanted to let me know he was doing well and thought I would want to know that. I was in the middle of writing this chapter, with a self-imposed deadline looming nearby. I saw who was calling as I reached for my cell phone, and immediately I felt the Spirit remind me that this young man was more important than a book. I answered the phone call with a smile on my face and enjoyed our time together. Isn't God good?

The fifth and sixth lessons learned were *present growth opportunities for your spiritual sons and daughters* and *allow for failure, because failure is a great teacher!* I got my first leadership position in church at age 19. I was the Youth Pastor in a little Baptist church. I had been promoted to this position by Charlie against the counsel of some of the older people in the church. This opportunity allowed me to grow and fail wonderfully. Because of his confidence in me, I had the confidence to go ahead and attend Bible school to train for the ministry. I had no clue about what I was doing, but I had watched Charlie long enough to know some basics. Over time I got my own vision and strategy, and the youth group quadrupled in size. When I failed to prepare well, the evening went terribly. When I prepared well, it generally went well. Spiritual discipline came from experiencing failure; I will never forget that lesson.

Our seventh "absolute must" for fathers was *know God's perspective on who you are mentoring so the help you give is focused and Spirit-led.* Some of you might wonder how you get such knowledge. It's simple. Ask. Ask the person you are mentoring about their dreams and visions. What have past prophetic words indicated about their futures? Ask the Holy Spirit what He wants you to do during contact with them. The other day I had breakfast with two of my young ministry leaders. Before we meet, I always ask God what we are going to talk about. If He doesn't tell me, I just trust Him and go forward. I have a pretty good relationship with each of these young men and have some sense of what season in life they are in and what each might need. I hope I am never so arrogant to think I have something special for them every time we meet (I am just not that wonderful). But I know someone Wonderful who does have something, and if I am sensitive to His nudges I occasionally come off looking like E. F. Hutton to these guys.

Our eighth lesson learned was *don't take yourself too seriously.* No one else will, so why should you? I got this message myself during my first prophetic word at a prophetic conference in Spokane, Washington. Bill Friesen had me stand up and proceeded to tell me what had happened in our van on the way up to the conference. He told me that I was in a season where the Lord was playing with me; God wanted me to know that it was a precious season and I needed to relax and enjoy it. Bill advised me to stop taking myself so seriously. The word was delivered with a lot of love and it really hit home. It was all too true. I am still working on some of what he said. We too easily get wrapped around the axle because someone we care about is french frying his life. But we are not God. God is God! I like to teach people to picture themselves approaching the cross with Jesus standing in front of it, His arms open wide, ready to relieve us of our relationship burdens. When you approach Him, let Him hug you. Then give whoever you are worrying about to Him and walk around to the other side of the cross and sit down and rest up against it.

Lesson number nine is a combination: ***Some situations are best left to God, He will discipline those He loves,*** and ***some people are bent on self-destruction***. A father's influence is limited, but God's arm reaches as far as it needs to! We must realize that God is ultimately responsible for all of us. Spiritual fathers err when they fail to realize their limitations. We can find ourselves in messy situations where, as fathers, we think we have more authority and favor with those we mentor than we really do. One time I was in a mentoring situation trying to give advice when it wasn't wanted. I believed we had agreed that I could advise caution whenever I felt the need arise, but my "young apprentice" refused what I was offering and went off into the wild blue yonder. She has a very poor walk with God to this day. I had to let her go, and give her back to God. He disciplines those He loves (Proverbs 3:12).

In the world of mentoring or fathering, there must be boundaries. I teach the men I mentor that "God is responsible for x amount, the person you are mentoring is responsible for y amount, and you are responsible for z amount. Do not make your quantity bigger than their's or God's. Galatians 6 tells us to bear one another's burdens. A burden is something beyond what is considered a daily load. A daily load is working, feeding yourself, and providing your own shelter. A burden is something bigger than all of that. The Scripture tells us to let each take care of their daily load, but bear the burden with them. In fathering or mentoring, you must have discernment about what your role is and what it isn't.

We must learn to trust God with the people we are mentoring, even through tough circumstances. If you do, you will live to father another day. I have had several disappointing relationships as a mentor and one in particular was devastating. One young man I took under my wing had a ton of gifts and talents. He was good at almost everything he tried. Unfortunately, he seemed hell-bent on sabotaging his relationship with me. As I began to pursue him to help him understand his gift mix, he rebelled. He wanted to take charge of a particular ministry, but he lacked the maturity and gifting needed to lead there. Over time he began to send me email after email arguing about his rights and pointing out where he thought I was stupid and incompetent. Eventually he ended up leaving the church, in part because he felt he had burned his bridges with me. If I could have convinced this young man to get counseling, I think it would have helped him. Unfortunately, issues with his father spilled over into our relationship, and he left angry. The principles of reaping and sowing that we discussed earlier in this book have visited him, and sadly, he is now estranged from his own son. If I had continued to beat myself up over this failed relationship, I would not have the heart to continue to mentor. This young man is God's adopted son, just as I am. God is big enough to take care of the ones I can't!

The tenth lesson we reaped was *learn to please God* and *unlearn the need to please men.* If you get yourself in a situation where someone you are mentoring is rebelling against God, then you must, with a clean heart, be willing to speak even when it isn't appreciated or received. You will risk displeasing your son; accept the risk. You must ask the Holy Spirit when to speak, as well as how much to say. Many times you are God's voice when someone is about to make a huge mistake. They may be very compelled and committed to messing up their lives, and you need to be equally zealous "to speak the truth in love." In the majority of those situations into which I've spoken the hard truth, the issue has been a relationship. I have taught everyone I have mentored to always try to allow the Holy Spirit to define their relationships.

I can't tell you how many times I have seen a young man or a young woman french fry their lives by getting entangled with the wrong person. Years ago I had a young couple come to see me because they wanted to get married. In the course of the discussion, I detected a very large, red flag. I knew the young man did not love the young woman, but was pursuing marriage out of wrong motives. When I spoke to him privately, he denied it. When I tried to talk to the bride-to-be and her parents, they couldn't see it. Needless to say, my words were not pleasing to these folks.

I did what I thought was right in talking to all the parties separately, and then sought counsel from a friend who was on staff with me. He knew both parties very well and agreed with my conclusion. When we brought the whole group together, we asked the couple and family to put the wedding off for awhile so that the two of them could get individual counseling to prepare them to be stronger mates for each other. We felt that if they waited three to six months and received good counsel, they would have a better chance of making a very healthy couple. We felt that the wait would be good for them. In spite of our efforts, they married (elsewhere) and were divorced within their first year. My ministry partner had been mentoring the young lady when the young man came into the picture. Her emotional wounds were more of a driving force in her life than her desire for wisdom, and she paid a very high price.

It is easy to give up on people in the natural, but the Father's heart is to love, woo, and wait. I hope you are being challenged and inspired as you read about your call and destiny to father in the kingdom. Fathering is a noble, needed cause that requires a response from us.

Chapter 10

Spiritual Lessons that Season

*"And Jesus increased in wisdom and stature,
and in favor with God and men."*

Luke 2:52

Bringing Them Up Right

In this verse we can see some very important goals that a spiritual father will desire to see manifest in a spiritual son. In any discourse about raising spiritual sons, the fruit mentioned in this verse must be sought after. When a new convert comes into his salvation, he begins a process of understanding the dynamics of his relationship with God in very simple terms. As we covered in the first chapter, he discovers he is loved, and his sins are forgiven. Fairly quickly after salvation, character formation begins through teaching, the sacraments, and discipline. Along the way, the spiritual child discovers he has an enemy beyond his own flesh, and he begins to move on into the "young man" stage of spiritual development. In this stage he learns the Word of God and how to apply it in spiritual warfare on his way to becoming a spiritual father. Discernment becomes necessary as he seeks to overcome his own strongholds and those of others. ***Discernment is birthed in wisdom by listening to the Holy Spirit.***

As a believer grows in wisdom, he tends to grow in stature and favor. Wisdom is the key to becoming trustworthy; wisdom is the strategic weapon that enables you to overcome. For character to be formed in an individual, Wisdom must reveal Himself and the believer must embrace what He is teaching. The spiritual father must realize his job is to encourage sons to embrace, with faith, what God is doing in their lives. In recent months, I have come to the conclusion that there are more ingredients that go into the spiritual formation of a man than I am ever going to be aware of. In the remainder of this chapter, I want to discuss a few ingredients that I have found to be foundational.

First off, it is important that sons and daughters learn to *pray in faith*, because prayer is relational between the believer and God. A young believer must learn to trust God because he knows God loves him. I have a history of firing off all kinds of prayers without any forethought as to what I am saying. In the past I would have described my prayer life as "shooting from the hip" and hoping something worked out. I don't do that very often anymore due to some insights through the ministry of Graham Cooke. Allow me to illustrate my point.

Several months ago, one of our young people was diagnosed with brain cancer. Our church's prayer chain began to intercede on the young man's behalf. As we continued to pray, I became very dissatisfied with this process because I kept asking people what God had told them about the situation, and no one but his mom could give me an answer! She had told me that God had said He "was going to move mountains for her son" so he could get his healing. Truth be told, God did. Her son moved quickly through medical channels to the right specialists, and the surgeon was a Christian. During the operation, his surgeon needed a word of knowledge on how to remove the tumor, and he received it. The young man is fine today!

It is too common, in churches, for a tragedy to occur and prayer to begin without seeking God and His will for the situation. One intercessor may be binding the devil, while another is praying for divine healing. A third might be asking God for a quick end, while a fourth is asking God to give an open door to the best doctors. The lack of unity in prayer concerns me. To truly pray in faith, shouldn't we be unified before God, with knowledge of how He wants us to pray?

Today we gather leaders and intercessors whenever we have a tough situation, to first worship and listen. We ask God to tell us what He is doing in the circumstance we are facing. We then ask Him how He would like us to pray. We write all of this down on butcher paper. Once we have recorded the revelation, we piece it together into a prayer. Graham Cooke calls this "crafted prayer," the title of his book from which I learned this process.

Once the prayer is put together, we use it to pray daily for a designated period of time. It gives us great confidence knowing we are in agreement with God and one another as we pray. We know from the Scriptures that we need to pray in faith (Matthew 21:22). Graham Cooke says, "Prayer is finding out what God wants to do and asking Him to do it." Brilliant!

We had a situation occur a few years ago that highlighted a need for change in the way we approach prayer. A man in our church called me on a Saturday night and asked if he and his wife could come over to talk. My immediate inward response was, "Oh no!" I didn't want to have a counseling session the evening before church. (In my experience, you never know how long or messy the session may be.) In spite of my inward response, I invited them over. Just as I hung up the phone, the Holy Spirit told me they were bringing me a new vehicle. I was blown away. Pam and I had our moms and their women's prayer groups praying for a new van for us for a year and a half. Our old Suburban had been in the shop twice in the last ten days, and something else had conked out as soon as I had brought it home.

I quickly wrote down the date, time, and what God had said would happen in a little "detail" book I keep in my home office. I then told Pam who was coming over. I didn't tell her what the Lord had told me, but He fooled me and told her, too! So, Pam and I were keeping the same "secret" from each other. We both sat there fidgeting while we waited. Finally, after what felt like a lifetime, I saw a vehicle coming down our dirt and gravel road. In the cloud of dust, I couldn't see if there were two vehicles or not. As they turned into our little side road, I saw that there was just one vehicle. I was a little concerned that I hadn't heard God right, but thought I needed to wait to see what He was up to. When the couple came inside, the gentleman took very little time explaining to us that he and his wife had a check for a new vehicle for us. He apologized for not coming sooner because it had taken some time for his wife to sense God's will in the matter. I immediately told Pam to retrieve my journal from the study, and I showed everyone what I had written. It gave great peace to all involved when Pam shared that the Lord had told her the same thing.

After the excitement had waned, we spent some time talking about the future and the gentleman's concerns about having a lack of vision for what he was to do in ministry in our little church. Once they left, I asked the Lord why the gentleman had given us the money that night in particular, and the Lord told me that he had needed to do it then, because he wouldn't be able to do it later. I had an odd feeling about that reply. In less than six weeks, our friend was diagnosed with a strange form of cancer, and just a few weeks after that he died. I will never forget asking the Lord to confirm what He had said to me the night our friend gave us the money. All the Lord did was to quote this verse from Hebrews 9:27:

"And it is appointed for men to die once, but after this the judgment."

I had known in advance that my friend was going to die, though I didn't tell the church or my friend about my knowledge. The night he died, there was a large gathering at the home of an elder. I had been with my friend at the hospital earlier and felt the presence of the Lord in the room as I prayed. I felt the Lord speak into my spirit that it was good to pray for him and for his family gathered around the bed. But I couldn't pray for healing as another minister was encouraging me to do. It was a terribly awkward moment, because I didn't want to tell this pastor in front of the family that God was going to take our friend. Many of them weren't believers, and I knew it wouldn't help God's case with them if I said, "It is God's will to take him home." When I left the hospital to see how the group was doing at the elder's house, I was overwhelmed.

As I walked through the door of the house and listened to the prayers of our dear church family, some of them were saying goodbye to our friend while others were crying out for a miracle. What a mess! Needless to say, I felt like a "bad pastor" for not sharing what I knew and for not teaching the group to listen before praying. As I left, I told the prayer leader what I thought I had heard about the situation, and she confirmed to me that the Lord had told her the same thing. As I left, I told her to gently shut down the prayer meeting but to continue to worship God.

To be able to pray in faith, you need to be able to hear God's voice and to be open to accept the fact that His ways are different than yours. This man had been a lover of God and His people. I could write a list of "better candidates" for God to take home than this one. Yet knowing His will as we pray brings peace, hope and faith, regardless of how the circumstances turn out. As spiritual fathers, we need to teach our sons and daughters how to listen to God's voice regarding circumstances and then craft a prayer they can pray with endurance and confidence until He answers.

Along with praying in faith, we want to instill in our spiritual sons and daughters *how to be confident*. Hebrews 10:35 says:

"Therefore do not throw away your confidence, which has great reward."

Self-confidence isn't what I am talking about here. Instead, your confidence should flow from Christ in you and from your position in Him. This is an important aspect of confidence. If you are going to help your spiritual son increase in "wisdom, stature, and favor," he must have this kind of confidence. People who are growing up into spiritual fatherhood must develop character and confidence. If you do not truly grasp the significance of your position in Christ, then it will be difficult for you to be confident or to have confidence in anyone else. If you are a confident man, people will take the time to understand and believe in your convictions and vision. If you are confident, then you will likely be content. When you are content, you are stable. When you are stable, you are trustworthy. When you are trustworthy, people will help you with your ministry and vision. When people work together (think unity) there is much fruit.

Many times in my ministry I have felt depression or despair, but I have never felt defeated. I've learned that when things are hard, I need to draw on Jesus' love and the promises found in His word. After overcoming some of the things I have, I know that I can overcome any circumstance with Him as my guide. Jesus makes His strength available to us. Because He is with us, we can have all confidence. A man who is confident will continually grow because he stands on a foundation that can tolerate stretching. When you are insecure, you struggle with growth because the stretching process is so uncomfortable that you avoid it instead of embracing it.

When I was a young man in the faith, I felt like one of the most insecure people on the planet. I failed to confront sin and often found myself frustrated with the people God had put around me. Instead of going to the people that I had issues with, I gossiped about them to others on our team. Unfortunately, this led people to distrust me. Insecurity and gossip caused trouble I couldn't afford. I continued to struggle with this sin until I began to understand that I was loved unconditionally.

You will gain confidence when you establish your worth in alignment with God's perspective of you. When people tell me I stink, I check in with God before I believe them. If I really do stink, I get His strategy for change and cooperate with Him. I have counselors and wise people around me in my leadership team all of the time for this reason. When you have God's view of you, then you can look to Him for answers when situations are difficult, having confidence that you are loved and that He has an answer for you. When difficulties arise, it is always best to focus on God rather than on the situation. You can do that when there is no barrier of shame or rejection between you and Him. Confidence isn't the result of an absence of problems in your life. Confidence comes from being able to trust God with the problems you face, knowing that you are loved.

Confidence is built by integrity and character that please the Lord. John Paul Jackson teaches that when we have private victories overcoming temptation, we will be more trustworthy to God. I agree. When I wake up feeling like 500 pounds of sin on a Popsicle stick, I am in trouble. If I know that I am walking in sin rather than in the Spirit, my confidence in my ability to hear properly is broken. I also sense the chasm that comes between me and Him when I sin. Difficult situations are more easily given over to God when you have a clean conscience, realizing that He is a God of justice. If you created your own mess due to sin, He still works on your behalf, but you will struggle with your conscience and, therefore, your confidence as well.

You will become more confident if you refuse to compare yourself with others. I have mentored a variety of young men and women over the years. A common problem has been their compulsion to compare and compete with others. A wise spiritual father will not expect sons and daughters to be junior versions of himself. Nor will he expect spiritual children to be clones of one another in their gifting and anointing.

I have a friend, Tom, who seems to have favor wherever he goes. I have enjoyed his friendship professionally and personally, and our churches have done several outreaches, conferences, and classes together. One of the interesting lessons I have learned as his friend is that our roles and calls in the kingdom are different in spite of the high level of cooperation we have enjoyed. Tom has been given authority by a well known national ministry to oversee their Pacific Northwest Training Center, and he also sits on the Board of Directors of a related organization.

My call is obviously different. I seem to do well outside of the United States in doing pastors' conferences and crusades. Though I admire and respect Tom, I am not Tom and shouldn't expect to have the same vision, purpose, and ministry life. Likewise, when we mentor, we can't expect that our sons and daughters will do the same things we have. It is our job as mentors to help them to be their best according to their unique gifting and calling. If I coveted what Tom has, I would miss what I have. That would grieve the Father. If you long to make a bunch of people into "junior you," that would grieve the Father. If you desire to be just like your mentor, you will be greatly disappointed. Comparing, contrasting, and competing are dead end roads. Teach your sons and daughters to avoid this at all costs. Those who want Scriptural evidence of what I am talking about just need to go to Genesis 4 and read about Cain and Abel. Jealousy and competition lead to spiritual (and sometimes physical) death.

As a mentor you instill confidence in your sons and daughters by loving them and helping them do well in the tasks you give them. As you model God's love to them and speak positively about their abilities while you help them grow and improve, they will blossom.

Having discussed the significance of the prayer of faith and of confidence, I'd also like to stress the importance of *learning to love*. In the Bible we are told to "love our enemies" (Matthew 5:44), to love one another, and to love God. I figure if we can accomplish these three things in our lifetimes, we will have done pretty well! I once heard a prophet share that he had become very ill, died, and went to heaven. When he arrived at the gate, he was asked if he had learned to love. Evidently learning to love is important up there!

Those whom I've mentored over the years know that I like to teach young people how to live for God and how to love others. As my spiritual dad, Tom Miller, likes to remind me, a father's job in a family is to "call the children out to life." If we sit in our booth at Denny's long enough, eventually one of the young people will get around to asking how to deal with a particular problem he is having. Whether an issue is personal or related to ministry, a mentor primarily reflects the Father's heart into that problem or situation. There isn't anything else. Once you understand that, you can prepare to be a good listener and help them find God's heart and a strategy that leads to the potential for something good to happen.

Before you can teach someone to learn the way of love, you need to listen to them well. I know if I feel heard, I am much more apt to listen and receive help. I believe most people are wired the same way. A mentor should do a lot of listening. Your sons and daughters need to feel safe enough with you to vent their frustrations. When you listen well, you offer acceptance and affirmation; hearts will soften and become open to a change of attitude and a better approach to a difficult situation. A good mentor will put his spiritual sons and daughters on a path to discover how to love in the situation by showing them how to get the Father's heart for the people they are frustrated with.

Allow me to offer myself as an example. I am by nature a verbal processor. My wife and friends know that I am passionate and opinionated. Knowing this, they tend to be Socratic in their approach with me, and when they do so, they win my attention. If they are harsh in the way they confront me, I tend to dismiss them. Not everyone is as temperamental and difficult as I am, but many are. When we are fathering others, we need to respect their anger or frustration, waiting for the right moment to nudge them into discovering God's perspective.

When you teach about learning to love, emphasize faith, hope, patience, and grace. When I am wrapped around the axle over something, my wife lets me blather and then asks if I might need a little bit of a perspective change to be effective when I "minister." Upon evaluation, I usually find that my anger has moved me into a realm that lacks faith or belief in a person's potential, or I lack the grace needed to deal with the error they have committed. A quick flash through my own personal history usually cleans up my act in a hurry — if I'm the one doing the examination. If Pam tries to go there . . . well, let's just move on.

When you father people who are learning to father, teach them that with the presence of the Holy Spirit, they can operate at a higher level of maturity than they are aware they possess. That is why we call life in the Spirit "supernatural" instead of "natural." Spirit-filled or supernatural living is accessible because God is greater than our weakness and promises to show Himself strong in our weakness (2 Corinthians 12:9). When a young father begins to experience God's grace in life and in ministry, teach him that this is the grace God gives for kingdom ministry. If he understands that well, he should be able to extend grace to others when they fail to meet expectations. After all, he is walking in so much grace, he should be compelled to give it away. Besides, love is kind by nature (1 Corinthians 13:4).

The Bible tells us that love never fails (1 Corinthians 13:8). A father should consistently live out this message, which will create a safe environment for others to learn through failure. When your spiritual sons and daughters make mistakes, quickly reassure them with a clear message of unconditional love. Nurturing them with this type of love reflects the Father's heart best. When they watch you love well, they learn to love.

When we first formed Desert Rock, I became keenly aware that every decision we made was setting a precedent that others would build on later. How we treated people at the outset created a relationship philosophy that was foundational for the future of the ministry. Love is very powerful. In 1 Corinthians 13:13, the Bible tells us that it is the greatest gift of all. If our purpose is to get to know Jesus, to become like Him, and to take as many people with us as we can, we can bet that learning to love is the single most necessary ingredient to the makeup of a father in the kingdom. After all, I think I read somewhere that God is love.

I want to close this book with a note that one of my spiritual fathers sent me today. I hope it encourages you as much as it did me. I thought the timing of this was amazing. I think our Father in heaven has a similar message for us all.

Steve,
It is well known that the Father's job in the family is to call the children out to life. Calling them out from the mother and training them with life's skills. I believe that the Lord is saying to you that you are such a spiritual father. You are being raised up yourself to call people out from their early salvation experience to a more refined and skillful life to be able to see babes born into the Kingdom and then call them out to more powerful and effectual lives for Christ. That is the word for you today in my opinion. Still, remember that I am just a sinful man reborn through the powerful blood of Jesus.

T. Miller

Appendix

Tools for Mentoring

It is my sincere hope that this list of tools will help you help yourself and others along the path to intimacy with God. I have put together a list of ministries for healing, and growing in the prophetic, as well as a list of books you might use to mentor others. I am sure I have missed things that are worthy and I don't pretend to be exhaustive in my approach. I simply listed the resources that I have found helpful in my walk with God and with helping others.

I believe you should be able to find the majority of the books and CD's I list on the web at Streamsministries.com or your favorite bookstore. If not, do a little bit of "Googling" and you should be able to come up with what you are looking for. I have made some comments by some of the resources and have said nothing about some of the others. All of the sources are worth your time. I hope you are blessed.

Healing Resources

Elijah House Ministries
Spokane Valley, Wa. 99206
509-321-1255

This ministry was started by John and Paula Sanford years ago and is still one of my favorite places to send people who can use some counseling help. The structure is such where you can go for a week and get a ton of healing at a ridiculously low price. I highly recommend them. We have referred dozens of people there over the years with outstanding results.

Rebuilding Lives Christian Counseling
Rob Morrissette
157 Hayden Ave. Suite 204
Hayden, Idaho 83835
208-762-9770

Rob spent years as a staff counselor and eventually the counselor's overseer at Elijah House. He is the one that God has used on a couple of occasions to put me back together when I have crumbled. I have a very high view of Rob and his skills. He has counseled numerous pastors and has a book called *Pray Through It* that is a must read for those who need healing or are in the healing business. His website is *www.RebuildingLives.cc*

Training Resources

Streams Ministries
John Paul Jackson/Patty Mapes
www.streamsministries.com

Streams Ministries was founded by John Paul Jackson, and Patty Mapes oversees the Institute for Spiritual Development. The classes they offer are called: The Art of Hearing God, Advanced Prophetic Ministry, Reaching Your Destiny in God, Understanding Dreams and Visions and Advanced Workshop in Dream Interpretation. I have both taken and taught these courses and they have changed my life immeasurably. Most of my current church has taken "The Art of Hearing God" and many have taken all of the courses. I highly recommend that you consider looking into bringing these courses to your church if you pastor. The issues dealt with in the classes help people develop respect for authority and the ability to discern their own strongholds. They also learn how to use their gifts appropriately.

I will never forget sitting in "The Art of Hearing God" and hearing the teacher talk about rebellion and authority. After hearing this teaching, I don't want anyone joining my leadership team until they have had this class.

Resources on Apologetics

Mere Christianity by C.S .Lewis

Trilogy –
The God Who is There
He is There and He is Not Silent
Escape from Reason by Francis Schaeffer

More than a Carpenter by Josh McDowell

Surprised by the Voice of God by Jack Deere (This is a must read for all of those who were trained Dispensationalists who want a theological framework to understand the relevance and use of the gifts today.)

Resources for Deliverance and Inner Healing and Healing and Self-Help

Pray Through It by Rob Morrissette
Transforming the Inner Man by John, Loren and Paula Sanford
Deliverance and Inner Healing by John Sanford
The Bait of Satan by John Bevere (this book saved me from major trouble!)
Overcoming Fear by Rick Joyner
Breaking Free of Rejection by John Paul Jackson
How to Pray for Healing by Che Ahn

Resources for Growing in Intimacy

Secrets of the Secret Place by Bob Sorge
The Secret Place by Michal Ann Goll (CD)
Experiencing the Father's Embrace by Jack Frost
God is the Kindest Person I Ever Met by Graham Cooke (CD)
Towards A Powerful Inner Life by Graham Cooke
Living in Dependency and Wonder by Graham Cooke
The Language of Promise by Graham Cooke
The Nature of God by Graham Cooke
God's Keeping Power by Graham Cooke

Resources that Train in the Prophetic and in Understanding the Ways of God

A Divine Confrontation by Graham Cooke (This book has unbelievable insight into change God's way.)
Books of Destiny by Paul Keith Davis
You May All Prophecy by Steve Thompson (this is so good for a home group to do together.)
There Were Two Trees in the Garden by Rick Joyner
Engaging the Revelatory Realm of Heaven by Rick Joyner
Open My Eyes Lord by Gary Oates
Hiddenness and Manifestation by Graham Cooke
The Seer by Jim Goll
The Priestly Bride by Anna Rountree
Pain, Perplexity and Promotion by Bob Sorge (this is an incredible prophetic look at the book of Job.)

Spiritual Warfare

Needless Casualties of War by John Paul Jackson
Unmasking the Jezebel Spirit by John Paul Jackson (both of these are necessary to pastor and lead people and for intercessors and prophetic types as well.)

A Tale of Three Kings by Gene Edwards (I didn't know where to put this book, but if you don't have your young men and women read this then you are failing them as a mentor.*)*

Prayer and Fasting

Crafted Prayer by Graham Cooke (This insight is so necessary today.)
The Hidden Power of Prayer and Fasting by Mahesh Chavda
Unrelenting Prayer by Bob Sorge

Resources for Living in the Supernatural

The Supernatural Power of a Transformed Mind by Bill Johnson
When Heaven Invades Earth by Bill Johnson
The Beauty of Spiritual Language by Jack Hayford

Evangelism

Prophecy, Dreams and Evangelism by Doug Addison

Resources for the Budding Worship Leader

Facing the Wall by Don Potter
Exploring Worship by Bob Sorge

Resources for the Budding Missionary

Always Enough by Heidi Baker
God is Bigger Than You Think by Heidi Baker (CD)

Discussion Questions for Small Groups

Chapter 1

1. What are the three stages of a Christian's maturity process?

2. What stage do you see yourself in and why?

3. What significant lessons have you learned in your current stage of development?

Chapter 2

1. In your walk, what has God taught you about your heart and His?

2. How has God changed your heart in the past?

3. What events has He used to shape or conform your heart to His?

Chapter 3

1. Which beatitude is your favorite, and why?

2. Share a story of when God brought you into a greater understanding of a particular beatitude/attitude.

3. Which beatitude sticks out to you as an area where you need improvement? Pray for each other concerning growth in these areas.

Chapter 4

1. When did you first become aware that you were hearing God's voice?

2. Have you ever been afraid that you might be deceived by the enemy instead of hearing God's voice? Look up Luke 11:9-13 and discuss it.

3. Share a time when you lacked discernment, or when you had it! What did you learn about yourself, God and people in these experiences?

Chapter 5

1. Share a time when you knew you were offended and how God helped you get healing.

2. Have you ever been persecuted? How did you handle it?

3. Think of a time when fear had power over you. Share how you overcame it.

Chapter 6

1. Have you ever felt trapped in an addiction or behavior pattern that seemed too large to overcome?

2. How has God "broken" strongholds in your life?

3. Is there a current "stronghold" that you could use prayer for? Pray for each other.

Chapter 7

1. Can you think of a time when you felt like you were all alone facing a "giant"?

2. How did you overcome the "giant"?

3. What have you learned about strengthening yourself? What tools do you use to do it?

Chapter 8

1. If someone were to ask you what your purpose in life was, what would you say?

2. Have you ever found yourself straying from your purpose?

3. How do we typically get "off course"?

Chapter 9

1. What tools do you need to parent or father in the natural and spiritual realms?

2. Where do you struggle most in parenting or spiritual fathering?

3. Who has been a good role model in your life? How have they done this?

Chapter 10

1. How important is having "favor" in life?

2. How does being wise affect favor?

3. How have you learned to be confident? Do you currently lack in confidence? Why? Pray for each other about this.

About the Author

Steven Watson (BA History/Philosophy - MA Counseling) is the founding pastor of Desert Rock Fellowship, in Richland, Washington. Steven started in ministry in 1979 and has been involved in numerous church plants, while also training close to 1000 pastors and Bible school students in India and the Philippines. He has done healing crusades, taught, and counseled for many years. Steve lives with his wife Pam, and their four children in West Richland, Washington.

To request Steven for conferences and other speaking engagements or to order more books contact:

Steven Watson
Desert Rock Fellowship
1916 Jadwin Avenue
Richland, WA 99352
Website: www.drf-church.org
Phone # 509-943-1445 or
509-967-1345